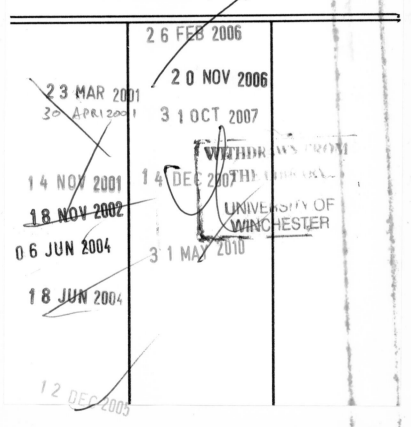

The Timber-frame House in England
in England

Pattyndenne Manor, Kent

The Timber-frame House
in England

Trudy West

photographs and drawings by Paul Dong FJI

David & Charles : Newton Abbot

ISBN 0 7153 4979 1

Set in 11 on 12 point Garamond
and printed in Great Britain by
Latimer Trend & Company Limited Plymouth
for David & Charles (Publishers) Limited
South Devon House   Newton Abbot   Devon

Contents

List of Illustrations

In Text

Preface

The fascinating history of timber-frame houses is to be found not so much in contemporary records as in examination of the attractive houses that remain. We have set out to record this history as lovers of old buildings and fine craftsmanship. We wish to pass on this interest and to supply information to those who want to know what they are looking at, how it was constructed, and how to distinguish the genuine from the false. We hope this book will also help the growing number of people who want to restore their homes to their former glory and supply some of the answers to those who are contemplating buying timber-frame houses, old or new.

The text is not technical, except where such information is necessary. The full technical details of many of the buildings mentioned are to be found in the specialist proceedings of various archaeological societies and such organisations as The Society for the Preservation of Ancient Buildings.

The main theme of the history of the timber-frame house is the sheer durability of timber. One has only to see the wonderful stave churches of Norway, which have stood for 800 years, to realise that their timbers are as near impregnable as anything can be. As with old timber houses, all the parts are joined together in a flowing unity to give elasticity with toughness, so that the building will yield slightly to the stresses of storms but will never break. This was proved during the bombing attacks of World War II, when timber-frame houses seemed to shiver under the onslaught and then settle down, whereas brick houses collapsed.

Even now, timber has no equal as a building material. It grows in large quantities and will keep on growing providing that man adopts a sensible plan of reafforestation. It presents no greater fire hazard than other materials, nor is it any more susceptible to pests or infestation as long as the necessary precautions are taken. The large numbers of partly neglected buildings still standing from the Middle Ages are witness enough to timber's long-lasting qualities.

We have seen all the buildings mentioned in this book, and though they are not necessarily open to the public they are all visible from public roads, with the exception of two modern houses. Wherever possible, we have examined buildings actually lived in and not merely preserved as tourist attractions.

Much that appears to be timber-framed is only brick or some other material with timber decoration, so we have defined a timber-frame house as a building with a frame that is self-supporting, carrying floor and roof timbers, from which it would be possible to remove all other materials without the structure collapsing.

ONE

The Story Begins

The story of architecture records all the changes in a nation's social and economic conditions, and reflects the cultural and intellectual progress of the people in a way that no other medium can, because it is so closely related to life. Although timber building is but a fragment of the story, it deserves a far more prominent place in history than it has yet been given.

More than any other form of building, timber-frame construction has its roots deep in the past, so deep indeed that the first part of the story must come from the archaeologists. The story goes back to prehistoric times when the first settlers came to Britain, a land of dense forests and swamps with a cold damp climate that compelled them to seek warmth and shelter from the driving rain, snow, and wind. Then the most readily available building material was timber, torn roughly from the trees. With little regard for building techniques the people set about fashioning themselves a 'house' of sorts. It would have been virtually a roof, rising direct from the ground, a crude tent-shaped 'hut' built of a circle of poles tied together at the top with withies, and covered with brushwood, reeds, or heather weighted down by stones or turf to make a rough kind of thatch. It was not meant to be permanent, but just a shelter. In fact, circular huts built in similar fashion are still seen all over Europe, put up by shepherds, charcoal-burners, and others who need a temporary shelter or 'booth'.

The main drawback with such a wigwam type of shelter was the lack of room. No one would have been able to stand up except in the middle, and it was probably this great disadvantage which led to the building of a better kind of hut—oblong shaped, with the two sides of the roof joining at a central ridge, and the floor hollowed out from

6 to 18in. The earth was piled up all round the feet of the poles, which made a thick wall where it was most needed, and such an arrangement would certainly give the inhabitants more head room, if nothing else (Fig 4[a]).

At Farnham, Surrey, some hollows scooped out of the ground indicate the site of a cluster of shelters erected here by nomads as much as 6–7,000 years ago, and these have given the archaeologists some evidence for their theories. An even more interesting settlement has been found at Meare, near Glastonbury, Somerset, near the remains of a Lake Village known to have been inhabited in the Iron Age, about 200 BC. In this village there were wattle and daub hutments, bearing evidence of a crude kind of wattle made of any available materials like heather, brushwood, willow, or any pliable sticks, woven together and daubed with clay, which the weather would eventually harden. It is also obvious that by this date cutting and shaping of timber-frame walls and partitions and the tenon and mortise method of jointing had been discovered, and various well-made tools were in use. Moss was used as a kind of putty for plugging badly fitting joints and cracks in wood. There was a later discovery in the latter half of 1969, when archaeologists digging through the foundations of this Iron Age village found several well-preserved timber structures which gave evidence of much earlier occupation, possibly 500–1000 BC; according to their calculations even Neolithic occupation at about 2000 BC could not be ruled out. This was very valuable information, showing that these

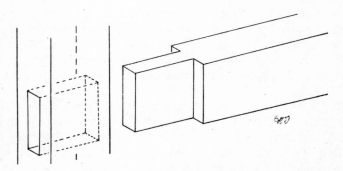

FIG 1   Mortise and tenon joint

prehistoric people had perhaps progressed faster than we had thought, and obviously used the same site again and again.

As man's knowledge increased he acquired greater skill in building and his communal meeting-places eventually formed the nucleus of many early towns and cities.

By the time the Romans came to Britain there were many light timber buildings with wattle and daub infilling, slender enough to fall easily to an enemy's axe, maybe, but homes rather than shelters. They were built in groups for protection against marauding beasts or men, and defended with earth banks, timber palisades, and ditches.

The Romans, with their superior methods of building frames of squared timbers with well made tools, soon began to erect new buildings and to improve existing ones. They paid attention to such details as site and aspect and they often built in two storeys. At first, the forests provided their materials which they used with a scientific precision which commands our admiration to this day. Colchester was the first Roman colony in Britain and there is much of interest to be seen there; and the remains at St Albans (Verulamium) are also a good example of early timber-frame construction, the frames there being erected on wall plates bedded on dwarf masonry walls to keep the wood from rotting in the ground. As the Romans began to widen their knowledge of materials, or as these became more readily available, the ground floor was sometimes built entirely of masonry with the upper floor timber-framed. At first, thatch was used for roofing, but when the danger from fire became too great the Romans used stone slabs, or they burnt clay from the fields and made tiles and bricks. The Roman tegulator, or tiler, was a valued craftsman. In places where the army did the building the tiles were marked with the number of the Roman legion concerned. In these cases it is possible to date a site, because we know the movements of the legions from other sources.

The legions built fine wooden villas with many rooms and surrounding verandas, and topped them with red-tiled roofs supported by wooden posts. One of the earliest buildings discovered on the Roman site at Bignor, Sussex, was a timber-frame house, built about the end of the second century. It was later destroyed by fire and rebuilt in stone, but the archaeologists were able to verify the existence of the original building by the traces that were left.

After the collapse of Roman rule in the early fifth century came the semi-barbarian Angles, Saxons, and Jutes from the forests of Denmark and Northern Germany. Timber was their natural building material—they knew no other. They were not town-dwellers, and the Roman towns were soon left sacked and deserted. They preferred their traditional ways, settling into villages of their own making, and the great forests and oak woods of Britain soon began to be perceptibly thinned under their axes.

Though the homes of the poor were no more than mud hovels, the more important farmers built themselves barn-like halls, often some 30–40ft in length and about half that width, timber-framed and thatched. It has been said that their basic plan differed little whether building for church, man, or beast. So the 'hall' had aisles divided into bays—one or more providing accommodation for the animals and the men who looked after them, another bay for the hay and the grain, and another, slightly better, for the farmer and his family. Privacy was unknown, for the Saxon (a general word, including Angles and Jutes) was essentially a farmer, content to live in earthy proximity with his herds and his retainers.

At some stage the owners of these barn-like halls turned the cattle out into byres and the hall became a house of sorts, with a fire on the beaten earth floor in the middle. Possibly a long timber hall of this class would be enclosed within a palisaded courtyard. –

We know that the early Saxon buildings were wooden from the writings of the Venerable Bede as well as from the records of archaeologists, and until the end of the sixth century each Saxon farming village had its hall; many traces of them have vanished. Greensted in Essex has a unique survival in a Saxon wooden church, dated to 1013; it is said to have the oldest wooden walls in England, made of split oak trunks. Although the building was re-fashioned in the sixteenth century and some additions made, it is still essentially Saxon.

From time to time some remnants have been unearthed that enable us to reconstruct in theory some of the very early Saxon huts. A 1968 excavation at Holbeach St John's, Lincolnshire, under the direction

Plates I and 2 Exterior and interior of Hunter's Cottage, Houghton, Hampshire

of Mr David Kaye, revealed some stake holes that gave the archaeologists a fair insight into the size and shape of the building, and
various finds helped to build up a picture of the superstructure. On
the evidence from pottery and from the clay droveway, the hut could
be dated to the third or fourth centuries. It was situated upon an
apparently natural mound about 6ft above the surrounding countryside. The walls were supported by stake posts, sunk up to 6in
through the 3in thick clay platform on which the building stood (see
Fig 2). Considerable amounts of daub were found, some of which
had burnt fragments of birds' bones mixed with it. Tiny pieces of
pigment found along the line of the inner face of the daub indicated
that the interior walls of the hut had been painted dark red. The
platform itself covered an area of 176 sq ft, while the hut's area was
approximately 88 sq ft, and there were signs that a partition had
divided it into two unequal size rooms. No hearth was found, but
there was a natural stream for a water supply and a drainage ditch had
been dug at the foot of the mound. When excavated this ditch filled
up with a depth of 6in of water to a width of 2ft 6in. Only one iron
nail was found, but other finds included several pot-boiling flints,
three particles of clinker, and a Belamite phallic symbol. With a
little imagination it is possible to build up a picture of an early
habitation such as this one, which probably had more amenities than
we suppose.

Another excavation made near Seaford, Sussex, during 1968 revealed the post holes of a large Saxon timber building within a
cemetery, with the remains of several huts nearby. From this it is
natural to deduce that there was a temple in the burial ground with
the villagers' huts close to it.

Most of the common people of that time would have lived in
similar wooden buildings, with a roof supported on posts and having
walls of interwoven osiers plastered with mud. In the centre was the
open fire with the smoke escaping through the entrance or through
gaps in the thatch. The window, or wind-eye, was no more than a
hole in the wall, made for ventilation or lookout and covered when

Cruck houses. Plate 3 (*above left*) Harwell, Berkshire; Plate 4 (*above right*) Much Wenlock, Shropshire; Plate 5 (*below*) Weobley, Herefordshire

B

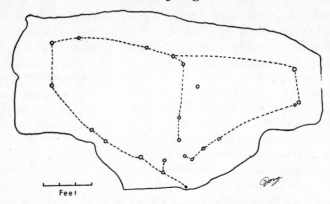

Feet

FIG 2   Plan of third-century hut, Holbeach St John's, Lincolnshire

necessary with a rough lattice of wattle. These small huts clustered tightly together in the shadow of a big house or monastery for protection, for they were vulnerable to any kind of enemy.

Although the Saxons were generally crude unimaginative builders, their carpenters showed some skill in the use of timber. They undertook everything to do with the building of a house, from the felling of the timber to the making of tile pins and pegs. The trees were felled and sawn up with a double-handed pit saw, one man standing in the pit over which the tree was placed and the other standing above it, and between them pulling the blade up and down. Small wonder that the man in the pit was known as the underdog! For all this, the sawyer was a very important man in the Anglo-Saxon community. He soon mastered the art of sawing the timber into shapes and sizes, squaring it and facing it up with an adze, following the fibre of the wood as he did so and making the finished effect as smooth as if a plane had been used, yet leaving a pleasantly undulating surface to the timber. He learned to use the chisel and the auger, to make mortises and tenons, and to pin the joints with strong wooden pegs of heart of oak. Thus he graduated from being an ordinary sawyer to becoming a fully fledged wright, the professional house-builder to the village and no doubt well paid for his work.

When he had squared off his timbers for use as beams he was left with some rough planking which he used to cover the roof rafters;

the remainder he split into shingles, cutting them by hand so that the grain of the wood acted as a conductor for the water. The Saxons protected the wooden walls of their best buildings with such shingles, pointed or rounded in fish-scale effect, and they also covered their steeply pointed roofs with them, overlapping them in a neat pattern, as the most effective method of weatherproofing they knew. This style of building is seen in the Bayeux tapestry, and even when the Saxons built in stone, towards the end of the period, they still simulated the designs of their earlier timber work.

In his book *Old English Houses* Hugh Braun reminds us that 'the principal contribution of the Anglo-Saxons to the timber building craft in this country was undoubtedly their introduction of the "ground sill". Prior to this, the native builders would have planted the poles of their houses in the earth, a bad practice as water would rise up the end grain of the timber to rot it where it emerges from the ground. From this time onwards the ground sill remains as the basis for all timber house construction'.

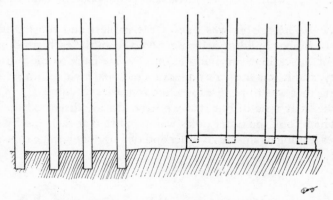

FIG 3   Posts in ground and ground sill

When the conquering Normans came to England in 1066 they brought with them some new ideas. It is said that they brought timbers cut and shaped ready for fixing, and erected their first 'motte and baily' (moated and walled) castle of timber and earth at Hastings immediately on landing.

Although the Normans were essentially builders in stone, timber was their principal building material in those areas which were thickly forested—particularly in the north-west, where a great forest covered the counties which we now know as Cheshire, Shropshire, Hereford and Worcester—and this practice lasted for some hundreds of years until the forests were exhausted. Even forts and castles continued to be built in timber and earth in this area for about 150 years after the Conquest. But on the whole very little is known of Saxon and Norman timber-frame construction because so few remains have been found. We have to rely on documentary references and old drawings to help us to visualise these early buildings.

The Norman nobles protected their forests only for hunting, and timber was generally regarded as an expendable and readily available material. Fine oak was ruthlessly chopped down and used impartially for building, smelting, charcoal-burning, domestic heating, and cooking as well as innumerable other purposes. There seems to have been no attempt to replace the fallen trees and no thought for the future. They were probably misled by the apparent gain in arable land.

Cruck Building. This was one of the earliest and most primitive forms of timber building which evolved from the early kind of hut. Some of the earliest surviving examples date back to the thirteenth century, and it was the forerunner of a national style of timber-frame building that was to persist for some centuries to come.

In the early type of hut that we have already discussed the ridge pole which took the rafter poles was supported at each end by a pair of poles leaning against each other and tied together at the top. These

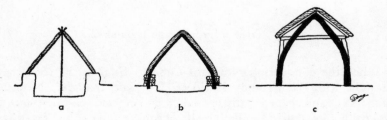

FIG 4   Development of cruck frame

pairs of poles, one at each end of the hut, gradually assumed more importance and became part of a definite design, so that instead of straight struts, naturally bent timbers were used, each pair formed from the split halves of the same tree trunk. Placed in reverse they formed an arch, or a cruck (see Fig 4[b]), or a style (in some localities). Sometimes the two halves met at the apexes, or they may have been crossed, fork-wise, to take the ridge pole or roof-tree. Each pair of crucks was usually reinforced by either a cross beam pegged into each member to give it greater stability, or by arch, scissor, or other braces. The building at this stage must have resembled an upturned boat, with sloping walls and very little headroom inside. The quaint little Teapot Hall in Lincolnshire was a good example of this inverted V type of building, made solely of sloping timbers, but unfortunately it was destroyed by fire in 1944 and exists only in photographs. Its appearance was not unlike a modern A frame. It was not in fact an authentic survival of this primitive tradition but a very good later imitation.

As cruck construction developed and buildings increased in size the division between the wall and the roof became more definitely marked by the angle of the curves of the crucks. In order to give a greater spread to the roof and more room inside the house, the tie beam at this point was lengthened to the vertical line of the base of the crucks and connected to the base by posts (see Fig 4[c]). Wall plates were then placed on the projecting ends of the tie beam (sometimes referred to as a 'spar' in old manuscripts) which extended between pairs of crucks, forming a stout surface on which the roof rafters rested, and vertical wall was built beneath these plates. At first these cruck houses were erected without foundations, with the ends of the timbers charred in an effort to preserve them, but later a rough stone base or timber ground-sill was found to be more practical.

The space between the two pairs of crucks was known as the 'bay', open to the rafters, and the humble one-bay cottage was the normal home of the labourer and his family, in all probability shared with the animals. Even the larger halls were shared by whole families, servants, and animals. The fire was either on the beaten earth floor or on a flat iron pan in the centre of the room, the smoke escaping where it might.

When Bishop Hall wrote: 'Of one bay's breadth, God wot! a silly cote, Whose thatched sparres are furr'd with sluttish soote—' he was without doubt referring to a primitive construction of this kind.

For family living it could be extended by one bay or more, to make a long house, cruck building being the most practical way of building a range of single-storey buildings.

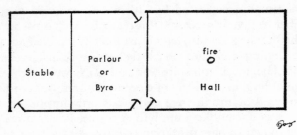

Stable

Parlour
or
Byre

fire
O

Hall

FIG 5   Early cruck house (plan)

Welsh cruck building is the best in the remaining examples. The records of the Radnorshire Society show that this type of roof structure was common throughout the county, with cruck trusses found in most forms of house from the humblest cottage to the most ornate 'Hall'. The *Records* say: 'The dating of the cruck house is difficult. The earliest surviving cruck-trusses date back to the 13th century and continued being used right through to the 17th century.' They point out that one factor that helps in dating this type of truss is the type of joint used between collar-beam and cruck. The cruck was mortised to take the tenoned collar-beam until the mid-sixteenth century, but from then on it was usually replaced by a lapped joint. The main advantages of using the cruck are that it gives a good room height providing large enough crucks are used, even without tie-beam and posts; and it is self-supporting, directly transferring the weight of the roof to the ground, which makes it particularly suitable for timber-frame building.

Some of the late cruck houses were found in the Midlands and most of them were of two or three bays. The traditional cruck-built peasant house in West Yorkshire and Lancashire usually consisted of three bays.

This type of building was once general in south-east England, before it was replaced by more advanced techniques. One must assume the former existence of cruck houses that can no longer be seen, for guide-books often refer to examples which have since been replaced or heavily disguised by an outer skin of brick or stone, or an extension. Nevertheless, there are some genuine survivals still to be seen if one is on the lookout for them.

Visitors to the picturesque village of Weobley, in Herefordshire, cannot fail to notice the well-restored black and white building behind the *Red Lion*, with its great natural cruck, probably thirteenth century, in the gable end with two diagonal struts above the collar-beam (see Plate 5).

In Much Wenlock, Shropshire, there is a less massive type of cruck, reputed to be fifteenth century, where the timbers bear more resemblance to an inverted V (Plate 4); and farther south, in Berkshire, the mid-fifteenth-century Dell Cottage in Harwell (Plate 3) has a cruck end with an added gable section, which gives this little thatched house an unusual but attractive appearance.

The idea that crucks were essential to support the weight of the roof died hard in many parts of the country and it was not until the seventeenth century that the framing of the wall and the roof were completely separated. Many of the crucks seen nowadays are in fact of seventeenth-century origin, put in to strengthen a timber frame at the gable end—ie the traditional gable fork. As a rule, the timbers are thinner than those of the earlier arched crucks, but they are none the less interesting as the latter form of this rugged and picturesque style of building.

TWO

The Manor House

The English manor house was an offshoot of feudalism, a system that influenced the character of English domestic architecture for some four or five centuries. This system was one by which men received their land from their kings and leaders on condition that they gave their services in war. Landholders were, in effect, little kings on their own land. They were nobles or knights, and their household servants and the peasants who worked their lands were serfs or villeins, for the whole feudal system rested on a substratum of serfdom.

Manors were formerly called Baronies and each lord was empowered to hold court, called the Court-Baron, with jurisdiction, criminal and civil, within the manorial territory. The Normans found this system with all its traditions of overlordship and community life, suited them very well and the Conqueror made few modifications to it. In the eleventh and twelfth centuries when the Barons were continually at war with each other, the manor house was of necessity a fortress, walled and moated, with a drawbridge over the moat, but the thirteenth century saw an improvement. England was becoming more settled under the feudal lords and barons and a greater feeling of security prevailed among the people. This rather more peaceful state was reflected in the general expansion of the manor house and an increase in the number of apartments in the fortified manors belonging to the clergy and the Crown, though during the reign of Henry III (1216–72) a great number of licences to 'crenellate' or fortify manor houses were granted.

The feudal system, already weakened by the Black Death (1349), came to an end with the Wars of the Roses (1450–71), for the powerful Barons had either killed or ruined each other and the country squires had become the 'upper classes', a fact which in itself heralded radical changes. But the event which had the greatest impact on architectural development in this country was the dissolution of the monasteries by Henry VIII. It was the final break between Church and Crown and it meant that for the first time secular building took precedence over ecclesiastical and the vast estates of the medieval church were distributed among people who had hitherto been without land. With the money and land which Henry VIII distributed among his courtiers many of them were able to build houses suited to their new rank and so become landed proprietors. This resulted in a complete economic revolution, releasing some of the finest builders and craftsmen of the day for exployment by others and making available materials which had once been the exclusive property of the Church.

In the Elizabethan age the manor house reached the height of splendour and extravagance, but in the following centuries it lost some of its importance. It was no longer involved with the government of the people and in the hands of the country squires it became just a symbol of an English way of life that was solid and dependable.

The manors we see today often span two or three historical periods, but the basis of the design of all of them is the hall. The aisled hall, or 'heall', of the Anglo-Saxons was similar to a church with an open roof supported on timber arcades, but in Norman times this became known as the Great Hall, a common meeting and sleeping place for all as well as being a court, a dining-room, a reception-room, and a theatre for strolling players. There seems to have been no limit to the functions of the Great Hall.

When the Norman lords began to feel the need for a little privacy they built flanking wings at each end of the hall, dispensing with the arcades except for the end pier, known as a spere truss, which marked a passageway between the hall and kitchens, or service wing. The spere truss held a 'screen', often beautifully carved, to conceal these quarters. In a large establishment the service wing might include a kitchen, a general service room, and a larder, where meat was preserved or 'larded'. At the opposite end of the hall, beyond the dais where the great lord sat, he often built a solar, or chamber, frequently on an upper storey with a cellar or storage room beneath it where he stored his valuables, and the way up to this solar was by a hazardous outside stair, or ladder. The effect was rather like a two-storeyed house with a joisted upper floor, and at that time it represented the height of comfort, a place of privacy and retirement solely for the use of the lord and his family. This hall plan is roughly the same for all

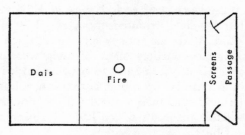

Fig 6   Basic hall plan

manor houses, small or large, and however much it has been altered or enlarged, the hall with its flanking wings will always be found to be the original part.

As the house expanded in succeeding centuries the hall remained the principal living-room and general dormitory for the household, the central fire providing warmth for all; but the stables and the lofts above them would also be used by servants. In some large houses the family apartments adjoined the hall, forming three sides of a quadrangle, with the rooms leading out of one another, but the smaller manor house now added a second storey to the rooms built at either end of the Great Hall, with gables at each end. The only way to reach these upper rooms was by means of a ladder, or probably a pine pole with pegs set into it at intervals. This gradually developed into a spiral stairway with solid oak treads turned into a central newel, but each wing was still cut off from the other by the Great Hall, which was open to the roof.

Although there is some mention of windows having been glazed in private houses as early as 1180, glass would have been a rare luxury and only seen in the houses of the great. It was the personal property of the owner and was not considered to be part of the building, so when the lord travelled he often took his window glass with him to be inserted wherever he stayed. It was too valuable to

leave unguarded and it was no doubt a status symbol as well. In the
reign of Henry III we read of painted glass windows with lattices
which opened and shut, but they were not English, for glass was not
made in this country until the fifteenth century; up till then it was
imported, but never in any large quantities because of its fragile
nature and the cost. For the sake of security these early windows
were set high in the walls and kept small and narrow, in the Gothic
style. Such small lights may have been glazed in part or filled in with
thin sheets of horn or oiled linen, to allow light to penetrate. It was
only later, when the country was more secure, that windows became
such a magnificent feature in the timber-frame house.

The typical large manor of the fifteenth century was moated and
built round three or four sides of a quadrangle. A gatehouse, a
portcullis, and a drawbridge were also necessary defensive measures.
Opposite the entrance a porch led to the Great Hall, with the kitchen
and numerous offices on one side and the family apartments on the
other. There was usually a short 'spur' screen inside the main door,
with a similar one to the opposite door, with possibly a movable
central screen to keep the draughts out. The screens passageway, as
it was called, was separated by two doors from the Great Hall or by
three doors where the kitchen lay beyond the service wing. Sometimes this passageway was covered over at first-floor level to provide
a minstrels' gallery overlooking the Great Hall, where some travel-
ling musicians might perform to the company. Even small manor
houses imitated this delightful fashion later on in the Elizabethan and
Jacobean eras.

The fifteenth-century Great Hall had become an imposing central
feature, with a magnificent open timbered roof lending an air of
dignity and solemnity to the proceedings of the manorial courts
which were still held there. At the upper end was the dais on which
stood the table of the lord and his immediate family or guests, and
below the great salt cellar sat the remainder of the establishment. A
canopy over the lord's seat marked its importance and there was
further embellishment in the enlargement of the window which lit
the dais, bringing into prominence its lofty position. This window
grew in importance and magnificence until it became the imposing
bay window which has since become a constant feature of English
domestic architecture.

The floor of the dais was made of wood but that of the common hall was most likely of beaten earth or clay, strewn with straw or dried rushes. Sometimes sweet herbs would be mixed with them, no doubt to counteract the stench of the refuse and dirt which accumulated, for the floor was the repository for every kind of garbage. Once or twice a month the whole lot would be swept up and replaced by fresh materials. For all the crudities associated with it it is a mistake to imagine the medieval hall as a gloomy place full of dark timbers disappearing into the recesses of the high, vaulted roof. On the contrary, it was more likely to be a colourful place, for the roof timbers and shutters were often painted in bright hues, the walls hung with painted cloths, arras and tapestries, for the ladies stitched zealously while their lords hunted or warred with each other.

In the smaller halls the same plan of building round a quadrangle was mostly followed and ornamental gables and porches were much in evidence. The growing desire for privacy towards the end of the fifteenth century led to the custom of the family dining in one of the smaller rooms. The private apartments gradually increased in number and the solar became the 'withdrawing room', or in Norman-French parlance, the parlour—a place for quiet conversation. Sometimes there was a second parlour under this room, on the ground floor, in place of the old storeroom. A lady's bower, or boudoir, was often provided next to the withdrawing room, serving the purpose of a best bedroom, for living-rooms were also used for sleeping until quite late in the age.

In larger houses there were now several bedrooms and a primitive kind of bathroom furnished with a laver came into existence. In the service wing, beyond the screens, were the kitchens (sometimes detached because of the possibility of fire), the buttery, the pantry and the larder. In a later age there was also a scullery, bakehouse, brewhouse, dairy, and possibly a mill, if there was a suitable water supply close at hand, as well as several outbuildings and granaries, so that a medieval manor house was virtually self-contained and self-supporting. It looked like a casual collection of buildings put up as and when they were needed, but the result was nevertheless attractive and delightfully spontaneous in effect.

The Tudor Manor House, though similar in design to that of the fifteenth century, was no longer fortified. Where a moat existed a bridge replaced the old drawbridge and a walled courtyard would only be necessary for reasons of privacy.

The Great Hall remained the central feature, but it lost some of its importance when the old feudal lords lost their power and its despotic functions ceased. During this period fireplaces became common and great chimneys were built. Now that the smoke no longer had to find a way to escape through the roof the Great Hall could be subdivided by the insertion of floors and partitions, to make a second storey and so increase the warmth of the house and the general comfort of the inhabitants. Great oak girders were thrown across to support the joists of the floor above and many ceilings were plastered between the beams. In the upper storey the open roof plan gave way to flat ceilings, some of which were ornamented and plastered; and so, with all this division and subdivision the Great Hall lost its air of majesty and mystery. In fact, it took on a completely new look, for the Tudors loved painted decorations and everything they could colour was coloured. They seem to have had no appreciation of the natural texture of timber or any other materials, for even the timbered ceilings we so much admire today would come in for a coat of colour wash.

In the early part of Elizabeth's reign there was a tremendous spate of building of all kinds as well as many improvements and enlargements carried out on existing houses. This largely accounts for the mixture of styles so often seen in old houses and confuses the tyro who is eager to put a date on everything. Nevertheless, it is possible to recognise features that were distinctive in a particular period, especially in manor houses. One is the kind of brick used; for bricks were becoming universally popular in the Tudor age, having been brought to England from the Low Countries. At that time the craft of bricklayer was added to that of the mason and the carpenter and the medieval 'house wright' no longer had the field to himself.

A typical early Tudor manor house may be a mixture of red brick and timber work, sometimes with the addition of stone. The ground floor may be built entirely of brick or stone with the upper floor timber-framed. Or the timber-framed structure may be nogged with brick, in which case a strong oak skeleton is set up and panels of brick laid between the members. The bricks could be laid in decorative patterns, either herring-bone or vertical, because they had no

bearing on the structure but simply served as an infilling to keep the
building weather-tight. Many earlier buildings had their wattle and
daub removed and replaced with bricks to follow the new fashion.

These early bricks were a good deal thinner than they are now.
They have always been about 9in long, but in Tudor times they were
barely 2in thick and were more like tiles. They were, of course, hand
made, burnt with wood fuel in a kiln or clamp, and roughly finished,
so that they made a very pleasing contrast in texture to the natural
grain of wood smoothed by the adze. The bricks were also laid in a
different manner from that of a later age. Before the reign of Queen
Anne (1702–14) they were laid in alternate courses, lengthwise and
across—technically speaking, in headers and stretchers, known as
the English bond. Later on, during the eighteenth century, a different
method was introduced, called the Flemish bond, whereby the bricks
were laid in headers and stretchers alternately in the same course,
breaking up the surface still more effectively (see Fig 45). It is easy
to detect these different methods in an old house, and it is one way
of dating it, or at least its period.

Another indication of age may be seen in the width of floorboards.
In late medieval times they were often 18in wide, and even in
Georgian days they were still 1ft or more wide.

Doorways were never quite such an important feature as windows,
the general idea being that they were primarily meant for the security
of the occupants. At first the frames were arch-shaped, then the hood
moulds over the doorways were made square, the triangular space
(spandrels) between the hood mould and the now flattened arch
often being beautifully carved. The typical early Tudor door is
framed in stout jambs, stop moulded and having a flat four-centred
arch. The heavy door itself may be made up of moulded and overlapping battens studded with nails and a large door or gate was
sometimes provided with a 'wicket' or smaller gate in or beside it
(Plate 12).

As houses grew in size so the number of gables increased, especially if the plan was H-shaped, and if a gable was big enough it
included a window. In general, the irregular groups of buildings
gave way to more symmetrical houses, with more attention paid to
comfort and convenience.

In the larger house many splendid features made their appearance, characteristic of the style and spirit of the Elizabethan age. First was the 'grand' staircase which replaced the former medieval steps placed in a turret at the side of the house. When the Great Hall was divided it meant that a number of important rooms were sited on the upper floors, which were no longer given over entirely to bedchambers. With the upper storeys linked together direct communication from one end of the house to the other became possible for the first time and a staircase to match the scale of the house was a necessity. At first, short straight flights were constructed in the form of a square which later developed into wide wooden flights with newel posts and balustrade, built round an open well. It was a very imposing feature, giving great scope to the joiner and designer, and the wood carver was able to use his skill to fashion some very fine newel posts.

A second great feature was the Long Gallery, which was always sited on an upper floor and made to run the entire length of the house. It was lighted by large windows and was very lavishly decorated with panelling and plasterwork. Its use has been questioned, but it was most probably designed for recreation and the enjoyment of music, or perhaps for gentle exercise in bad weather. Its main purpose was to house a 'collection' of some sort and certainly it would have been a picture gallery for the family portraits and even, on occasion, a dormitory when there was a great influx of guests. Whatever its purpose may have been it was a very popular addition to the Elizabethan great house where hospitality was of major importance and the hope of entertaining the Queen was ever present.

At this time formal gardens were incorporated into the general plan, with such additions as terraces, yew walks, and fountains. With the country peaceful the walled courtyard and gatehouse could be dispensed with, unless it was there purely for display. Although architects in the modern sense had not yet emerged, builders were beginning to see that a plan made beforehand produced better results. The former rambling 'Gothic' house now became more symmetrical, after the style of the Renaissance builders, assuming an E shape, with slightly projecting end wings. (This shape was not entirely meant as a compliment to the Queen as many have supposed.) The entrance porch was moved to the centre, the short arm of the E, leading to the main hall, the kitchens being on one side and the old living-rooms on the other. The hall had in this case become a vestibule. The servants no longer ate or slept there but had their own 'hall' for living-quarters. Some still slept in the kitchen, but by then there was space in the roof and beds were ranged down each side of the long low attics, which had generous dormers.

What has been called the Jacobean style was merely a development of the Elizabethan, externally symmetrical and dramatic, or as Sir Francis Bacon put it—'Uniform without though severally partitioned within'. Although there was more comfort and bedrooms began to be panelled against cold and damp, the designers still had no thought of providing space for privacy and the rooms continued to be thoroughfare rooms, one leading out of the other. There must have been much coming and going through bedrooms in those days but this was taken as a matter of course. To quote Sir Henry Wootton writing in his *Elements of Architecture* in 1624: 'They do so cast their partitions as when all doors are open a man may see through the whole House, which doth necessarily put an intollerable servitude upon all the Chambers save the Inmost, where none can arrive, but through the rest; or else the Walles must be extreme thicke for secret passages.'

Secret passages or no, the corridor for 'circulation' was a late invention and more often than not it was left to a twentieth-century owner to contrive such space and ensure privacy for the bedrooms.

It is seldom that we see a completely timber-framed manor that was built after the seventeenth century, though timber continued to be the main building material for smaller homes. It was in the fifteenth, sixteenth, and seventeenth centuries that timber-frame building took on an ease and grace which has never been bettered in any form.

The term 'manor', of course, embraces a very wide range of houses, from the grand establishment of the nobility to the lesser homes of the yeoman and the 'country gentleman'. It is impossible to list all the beautiful timber-frame manor houses which are to be seen in various parts of the country, but here are a few examples.

Farmhouses. Plate 6 (*above*) Moat Farm, Dormston, Worcestershire; Plate 7 (*below*), Synyards, Otham, Kent

Very few of the early medieval timber-frame halls are left to us, many of those in the north of England having been rebuilt in stone, but there are two very fine Great Halls in Lancashire—one at Rufford and the other at Smithells. There are others in Cheshire, at Baguley and Adlington. At West Bromwich there is an early Manor House which, as far as possible, has been faithfully restored to the original plan and is now in use as a restaurant. Known locally as 'The Old Hall', the buildings include a Great Hall, north solar wing, south wing, chapel, kitchen block, and gatehouse, the whole surrounded by a moat that is crossed by a bridge. The earliest part of the building is the Great Hall, which has been dated by the local experts between 1290 and 1310. The way into it is through a screens passage in which there is a central screen formed of very fine spere posts and trusses, in effect rather like a Gothic arch, with blocked-in screens at the sides. Because of this feature the Hall is generally supposed to be derived from a medieval aisled Hall, and is unique in that the central truss made the nave posts unnecessary and left space for a large gathering round the central fire. There is an unusual two-storey bay in the west wall which is thought to have been erected during the sixteenth century. On the opposite side of the screens passage are doorways with ogee heads, leading to the buttery and pantry, and a stairway to the south solar. The two cross wings—the north solar wing and the south solar wing—were probably added to the Hall in the first half of the fifteenth century, in place of earlier structures. An unusual sliding door gives access to the stairway up to the north solar; and both north and south solar rooms have some particularly beautiful roof trusses complete with wind braces, all original and in excellent condition. The Chapel, which was built at a later date for the use of the family, lies to the east of the north solar, and is generally regarded as being of incomparable design in this country.

The layout of the Hall differs from most in that the kitchen is placed at the upper end behind the dais and not with the other service rooms. There is, however, a separate kitchen block to the west of the south wing, which has been dated to 1500 or possibly earlier.

Plate 8 Reconstruction of medieval fireplace at Avoncroft Museum, Worcestershire

c

The Gatehouse has some interesting carpenters' assembly marks on the timbers, which are lavishly decorated on the front of the building but left plain, in panelled squares, at the rear. The whole building is now very well preserved and is worth more prolonged and detailed study.

In a different, more flamboyant, style is Little Moreton Hall in Cheshire, built in 1559, the most complete timbered mansion in the county and now owned by the National Trust. Access is by way of a stone bridge over the moat to the gatehouse, and like all other manors it was built round the nucleus of the original plan, that is, the great hall with the lord's chambers at one end and the service rooms at the other. Extensions were made in the sixteenth century, when the house became almost rectangular, built round a cobbled courtyard, and later additions included a gatehouse, a porch to the great hall, and two hexagonal bay windows, one to the withdrawing room and the other to the hall. The gatehouse wing contains the guests' hall, a parlour, and a secret panel concealing the entrance to two hidden rooms—probably priests' hideouts. On the top floor is the Long Gallery, which was added in 1602 during Elizabeth's reign, a very beautiful feature, but there are still no corridors and communication between the various parts of the house is not easy. The Great Hall was also subdivided at some time during the sixteenth century, but the dividing floor has since been removed, leaving the hall with its open timbered roof as it was first designed.

A fireplace was built in the north wall at the lord's end of the hall and a doorway leads to a staircase to the upper chamber. On the ground floor the lord's room is on one side and on the other is a fine panelled room with an unusual ceiling of heavy beams crossing each other to form squares, two moulded rafters facing different ways in each square.

Little Moreton Hall's complex timbering makes it one of the best existing 'black and white' Tudor houses in Britain. Externally, it is an outstanding example of the north-western style of elaborate diagonal strutting and quatrefoiled panels (see Chapter Eight) which continue in the gables and under the eaves. The chimneys are completely uncoordinated, for the fireplaces within the house were constructed as they were wanted, to no definite plan.

By contrast, Shoyswell Old Manor (Fig 7), in a sequestered part of

Sussex, is much less dramatic in appearance, but is still typical of a manor house greatly enlarged and modernised since Tudor days. It was mentioned originally in records dated 1296, when it was a moated house, built for defence. The moat has long since disappeared with nothing but a faint track to mark its original position, but an ancient well has been left in place. The original building was much smaller, probably little more than the Great Hall and some domestic offices. Now the Manor is a big imposing house, bearing many signs of its proud ancestry. The exterior combines close timbering, more widely spaced timbering, and hung tiles, but it all blends together quietly and unobtrusively, unlike its more exuberant north-western counterpart.

FIG 7   Shoyswell Old Manor

In East Anglia the manors are frequently plastered, so that it is difficult to detect the timbers at first sight. Tolleshunt D'Arcy Hall in Essex, a late fifteenth-century manor, is typical of this kind of building, so discreetly restored and modernised that it is scarcely possible to detect alterations. It stands in proud isolation on its own island, surrounded by a spring-fed moat crossed by a bridge which has brick piers at the entrance bearing the sculptured coat of arms of the D'Arcy family with the date 1585. At one time the manor was U-shaped, but the east wing was destroyed about 1789 and the south wing was rebuilt late in the seventeenth century. The main block, however, has so many original features left that one is able to build up a fairly accurate picture of the house in the great days of the

Tudors. A nail-studded door with moulded jambs and a carved lintel leads to a narrow stone-flagged passage running through to the back, where the remains of a typical Tudor arch can be seen and a staircase which probably replaced the early ladder-like one. This was the screens passage, which divided the Great Hall from the domestic offices, and at the back are two original doorways, with stop-moulded jambs, beautifully carved spandrels, and an embattled cornice (see Fig 39). These doorways lead into the dairy, buttery, scullery, kitchen, wash-house, brewhouse and other domestic quarters.

The Great Hall, where manorial courts were once held, is stone-flagged, with one wall panelled in oak and a door of linenfold panelling. It was once open to the rafters to allow wood smoke to escape through the roof, but the last Thomas D'Arcy built a huge brick chimney with the flue leading obliquely through an outside wall. The 10ft wide brick fireplace, constructed to take logs on the grand scale, has a chamfered oak lintel and niches in the side walls. This Hall was subdivided in the sixteenth century to make a second storey, and the stout beams which support the floor joists are in turn strengthened by a great post in the centre. The Hall is now used by the present owners as a family dining-room.

The main block is linked to the south wing by a library, a thoroughfare room leading to the entrance hall where there is some very fine early sixteenth-century panelling and an embellished ceiling (Plate 27). The withdrawing room is at the far end of the wing and its huge inglenook fireplace is built up through the ceiling to make another in the bedroom above. Tudor bricks are clearly discernible in the base, and a beam runs through the brick. The entrance hall has an imposing wide staircase, built to link the upper storeys of the two wings together.

Outside are Tudor dog kennels, timber-framed with brick infilling and built in eight bays; a sixteenth-century dovecot, having 691 nests; and a granary.

Apart from these large manors, there are many smaller manor houses which were built during the great Tudor building boom for the country squire and the well-to-do yeoman. Then the builders imitated the houses of the noblemen and produced these delightful timber-framed miniatures of the great manors.

Kent is particularly rich in this kind of house, since great forests
of oak once covered the Weald and the timber for building was
virtually on the doorstep. One of the best examples is near Goudhurst, where the owners have adopted the original spelling for the
name—Pattyndenne Manor (see frontispiece)—and have expertly restored and modernised the lovely old house. With its close timbered
exterior of oak studs and beams weathered to a silvery grey, and a
steeply pitched tiled roof, it looks much the same as it did when it
was built about 1470 and later owned by King Henry VIII's standard
bearer. Originally it consisted of an open hall, measuring 25ft by
19ft, with a screens passage at the north end, two service rooms
behind the screens, and a small parlour at the opposite end. There
may have been a small gallery above the screens passage, indicated
now by a tiny window high up on the east wall which would have
lighted it. Above, on each side, were two bedrooms, separated by the
open hall, and so a flight of steps at each end of the house was
necessary to reach them.

The roof of the hall is supported by two great main posts from
which spring massive arched supports carrying a carved tie-beam
12in wide and 16in deep and a crown-post (see Fig 8); the latter
supports a central purlin and collared rafters. Wide overhanging
storeys at each end of the house are jettied on all sides, the ends of
the projecting floor joists being concealed by moulded fascia boards.
At the corners of the building, the ends of the dragon beams are
mortised to the teazle posts on which they rest, the butt ends merging
with the ends of the dragon beams and carved in a simple decorative
form (see Plates 22, 23, and 24 for this type of construction). The
existence of these four corner posts and the jettied storeys at both
sides and ends of the building shows us the complete outline of the
original house. All other offices, including the kitchen, were built
later. Sometime in the sixteenth century a chimney stack was built
with its back to the screens passage, and a great oak girder was
thrown across the hall and fixed by mortise and tenon to the upright
main posts. Two secondary girders were added, one having its end
resting on the brick jamb, dividing the hall horizontally into three
floors. These girders and the joists are all richly moulded, as is the
great beam over the chimney opening. A wide oak staircase at the
back of the hall has replaced the original steps and a further flight of

steps leads up to the attic. Good oak-framed windows with transoms
and moulded mullions have also replaced the originals, which were
much smaller. Four stained-glass leaded lights in the hall window, of
which three are the badges of Henry VIII and Catherine of Aragon,
give a clue to the approximate date of the alterations.

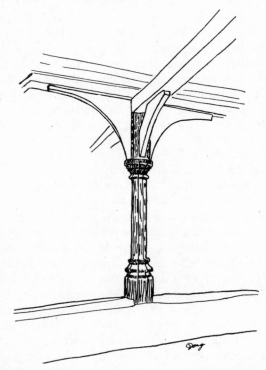

FIG 8   Carved crown-post, Pattyndenne Manor, Kent

This is typical of this kind of small manor, many of which were
originally granted as rewards for some signal service to the Crown
and they still uphold their dignity.

There was also a common type of manor house built in the West
Midlands around the mid-seventeenth century that had a hall range

and one cross wing, but these were very often the property of well-to-do yeoman farmers who could afford to keep resident workers. The medieval tradition of hall and cross wings, with a through passage and two opposing doorways, was the usual plan until the end of the seventeenth century. There were some variations, since timber-frame building is intensely individual and follows local designs, but the basic content and construction remain the same.

THREE

The Town House

Each period has given us something new in architecture to correspond with the social development of the times, and the town house is no exception.

At the time of the eleventh-century Domesday Survey there is evidence that small towns were beginning to build up in those areas which were good for trade, but the first important secular buildings were the magnificent Guildhalls (the first Town Halls) and Market Halls of the Merchant Guilds. In York there still stands the Hall of the Merchant Adventurers—a fine fifteenth-century building, where they sold cloth, and the Merchants of the Staple sold the wool. The very fact that buildings like this were subscribed to and built by the members of the Merchant Companies emphasises the rise in civic importance of the merchant classes in the Middle Ages.

The English town of the Middle Ages was dominated by the Church and the powerful Guilds, which also had a religious and charitable background. This influence is plainly reflected in the predominance of monastic buildings and timber-framed houses, which, by their symbolic carvings and decorations, show that they once belonged to one of the many orders of friars. But in the last analysis it is trade which attracts people to towns, and it was the wool trade, more than any other, which established England's commercial importance during the fourteenth century and changed the whole pattern of life for a vast number of her people.

By the time of the Tudors there was change and development in all strata of society. The great driving force of trade led to a proportionate increase in wealth and political power in London and other large towns, particularly the ports, for it was on their waterways that many historic cities built their greatness.

By the end of the Elizabethan period (1603) there were innumerable fine timber-frame houses to be seen, particularly in the Midlands, East Anglia, and the Welsh border towns, which were the equal of the country squire's manor house. It was at this time, and during the late seventeenth century, that some of the best examples of vernacular architecture appeared, but after this brick began to replace timber, especially in the towns, where the risk of fire made its use more prudent. Later, in the nineteenth century, when the Industrial Revolution filled the cities of Britain with ugly box-like houses built of mass-produced bricks, there were here and there a few Victorian clapboarded houses built for labourers, and some of these are still to be seen in the suburbs of London (Plate 9).

Building Regulations

They are by no means a modern innovation, and though it is difficult to trace their beginnings, they certainly go back to early medieval times. They did not apply so much to market towns, which seemed to develop around a Market Cross and Square, with buildings put up as and when they were needed, but there were stringent regulations in the big cities, which, with their close-packed timber houses, were constantly menaced by fire. London, with its seething population, was particularly vulnerable and had so many disastrous fires that some authoritative action became imperative, and so over the years a code of bye-laws was drawn up whereby certain rules had to be obeyed or the offending building was pulled down. The Aldermen of the City of London each kept a hook and rope for that purpose.

After the London fires of 1132 and 1136 the building regulations of 1189, brought in by Richard I, laid down that houses should have party walls 3ft thick and 16ft high, with alcoves of 1ft allowed into them, and overhanging gables and storeys were to be not less than 8ft from the ground. After the Great Fire of 1666, which virtually destroyed medieval London, a great part of the City had to be rebuilt and an Act was brought in which stated that all new buildings were to be made of brick or stone with similar party walls, and the old timber buildings gradually disappeared. Later, the London Building Act of 1774 prohibited the use of exposed timber details on buildings, but in spite of this, there are one or two reminders of the traditional style left, notably the row of old gabled buildings which form the front of Staple Inn, Holborn, and No 292 Strand, both of which are relics of the Tudor style.

We are reminded of the activity of medieval town planners in the Knollys Rose Ceremony, which takes place in London annually on Midsummer Day when the 'quit rent' of one red rose is paid to the Lord Mayor as a token of subjection for a breach of the City's bye-laws by Sir Robert Knollys in 1381. His wife had built a covered footbridge across Seething Lane to connect her house and garden, without permission, but a belated licence was granted to them, 'their heirs and assigns for ever' for the annual payment of one red rose. Infringement of the building regulations did not always meet with such leniency, for the houses were more likely to be pulled down, without redress.

Another aspect of town planning, when timber was getting scarce, is revealed in a seventeenth-century 'Proclamation' which is housed in the British Museum. It states:

> There hath been such a consumption of timber in the Realm that in the very City of London they are now driven to build with beech and other timber of small continuance which in time will be the notorious peril and decay of the city. It is now commanded that no part of a tree that may serve for any use of timber shall be converted to coal or firewood; and for the better preservation of timber, from the Feast of St. Michael no one shall erect any new house or the part of any house within the city and suburbs, except all outer walls and windows be made wholly of brick, or brick and stone. Moreover the forefront thereof shall be made of that uniform order and form as shall be prescribed, for that street where the building shall be, by the chief magistrates of the City.

Medieval Towns

Most medieval towns of any consequence were surrounded by stout walls, breached only by gates, strongly defended, and the smaller towns had stockades and ditches to protect them from attack. At first the space allowed for building within the walls was ample, in fact many plots allowed for large gardens to be included, but as the expansion of trade began to attract far greater numbers to the cities, more and more houses were built on what were originally intended to be single plots and the inevitable congestion followed.

According to social historians the townsman of the twelfth and thirteenth centuries lived in a house that was little more than a shed —consisting of one room that served as living-room and sleeping quarters—set with its gable end facing the narrow street. This was the general plan of all medieval houses, whether in town or country, the only difference being that in town the house was turned at right-angles to the street to fit the narrow frontage of the plot. The building must have been very insubstantial for an old document tells us that 'anyone who shall receive certain heretics shall have his house carried outside the town and burnt'. From this it is obvious that these poor little dwellings were not built on any solid foundation but were simply planted on the earth.

Building plots had rarely more than a 20ft frontage, and so the style of building was influenced by the restricted size of the plot, and the size of the plot by the walls of the city. One has only to take a close look at a city like York, for instance, where the walls are still very much in evidence, to get the true meaning of this limitation. Here the walls are 2½ miles in circumference, pierced only by four great Bars or Gates, and in the Middle Ages the entire population would be packed within them. Understandably, as a result of this kind of constriction, building land became scarce and valuable and the old familiar problems of overcrowding presented themselves. The problems are not new to us but the causes are different, and the solution was as obvious then as now—to build upwards; so England's first timber 'skyscrapers' made their appearance. By adopting the platform system (see Chapter Four) the builders were able to reach four or five storeys, jettied out one above the other, in tall top-heavy style. Their limited ground space compelled the houses to huddle together, giving each other support, with their overhanging storeys almost touching their neighbours across the narrow street in an enforced kind of familiarity. Their distinctive style typifies for us the English medieval town and as such has an enduring place in our affections, but from a practical standpoint these picturesque old houses owe their survival to the superb quality of their timbers and the fine craftsmanship of their builders.

These town houses were often roomy inside, and many of them combined business premises with living accommodation. The ground floor might be used as a shop, not entirely in the modern sense, but more as a room where the merchant displayed his goods and interviewed his customers. The 'shop windows', a little larger than the others and without mullions, had wooden shutters hinged at the top and bottom which formed a counter when they were open during the day and an excellent protection against thieves when closed at night. There are some examples of this type of medieval shop in the Market Square at Lavenham, Suffolk (Plate 15), where the shutters are still visible. The Abbot's House, Butcher Row, Shrewsbury, which dates from about 1450, also has a street-level frontage which houses a row of medieval shops in their original form, except for the later addition of glazed windows. There are still the wide oaken sills on which the shopkeepers displayed their wares, which, with the customers, were protected by the overhanging storeys above them.

In a shopkeeper's house such as this, there was normally a store room at the back, with a kitchen, a yard (which may have contained some kind of sanitary arrangement), and a stable. The first floor which jettied out above this 'shop' was the owner's hall, the second floor housed his chambers, and over them all were the attics in the roof for the use of his staff. A steep wooden spiral staircase at the back of the building led to the upper floors, though some had an internal ladder or open tread steps.

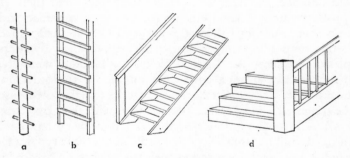

FIG 9   Development of staircase

By modern standards the towns were squalid and overcrowded, with poor sanitation and no proper water supply. Records seem to indicate that a few houses had cesspits, which were either in the yard or under the building, simply covered by loose boards. Those on the rivers' edge disposed of sewage and rubbish in that direction, sometimes through wooden drains. Brick drains were built later, though there was no sewerage system as we know it until the nineteenth century when Sir Joseph Bazalgette, CB, laid out London's main drainage system. These early drains usually served individual buildings only. Two early Tudor drains, one brick and one timber, were discovered in the bank of the River Wandle in Wandsworth, London, in 1969 by the local Historical Society, who investigated the site known as 'Stimpson's Buildings' during building works.

Medieval streets were little more than alleys, narrow and crooked, 12ft wide or less, with beaten earth, flat stones, or cobbles to form a road surface. Holborn, London, was first paved in 1415 and some of the streets of the capital were lighted with lanterns with glass sides, but this must have been something of an innovation. In general, the streets of towns only needed to be wide enough for the passage of carts, which left little room for pedestrians. Yet there was a good deal of colour in the street scene: some house fronts were painted or gilded, some colour-washed in pink or white or the more solid black and white, and some had beautiful carvings to enrich their beams for this was an age of good craftsmanship and design. For all that, the streets were noisy, crowded, and ill lit, and it was almost impossible for the air to circulate indoors or out. There is no doubt that the Black Death, which ravaged all classes of society in 1349, was due to cramped and unhygienic conditions in towns. By then, the population had increased to something like 4 million—three times as many as at the time of the Domesday survey. By the mid-fifteenth century London had between 50,000 and 60,000 people living within the city boundaries; a century later it was well on the way to having 200,000, which increased to half a million in the following 100 years.

The largest English towns at the beginning of the fifteenth century were London, York, Norwich, Chester, and Bristol, of first importance because of their great waterways and their positions on trade routes.

Fifteenth-century London was indeed one of the great cities of Europe, but the Great Fire of 1666 destroyed most of the old oak buildings and there is little left to remind us of that affluent period.

York is more fortunate in having kept intact the Shambles, which

typifies the narrow crooked streets of gabled overhanging houses of
that period in a remarkably authentic way.

Next to York, Chester is a good example of a walled city, built up
round a port on the River Dee. Its famous Rows are unique, forming
covered walks at first-floor level and continuing along the sides of
the streets to meet in the centre of the city, as they did in Roman
times; but unfortunately so many of the old buildings are nothing
but façades, extensively restored in the nineteenth century, that it is
difficult to trace any genuine medieval survivals.

Although the big cities have little of this period to show, the
smaller towns, having been less restricted, are worth studying. There
are still some tall jettied timber houses to be seen in towns like
Shrewsbury, Hereford, Ledbury, and Tewkesbury (Fig 10), but they
are fast being planned out of existence and one has to search for
them. Often the search leads to the rear of a building, where a
modern façade conceals the great posts and beams of a late medieval
house. Here we can see that the upper apartments were often
separated by boarded partitions, and the ceilings are the close-set
wide joists and boarding of the floor above. A glance into the roof
reveals the graceful construction of the trussed rafters, with curved
oak tie beams and wind braces which have withstood the elements
for many centuries and are most likely good for as many more.

The West Midlands is the most rewarding part of England to look
for old buildings, for this is one of the areas where trade flourished
in days gone by and the master drapers, weavers, and others built
their homes in the fourteenth and fifteenth centuries.

Some of the best examples of medieval building are to be seen in
Shrewsbury, described by Charles Dickens as a 'town of the crooked-
est black and white houses, all of many shapes, except straight
shapes'. It came into prominence with the Welsh cloth trade and the
prosperity of its merchants and tradesmen is reflected in the lavish
style of their houses, great gabled and jettied buildings with massive
close-set timbers ornamented with an exuberant pattern of black
beams on a white plaster surface, called 'magpie' to express its
startling contrast (Plate 35). The sunken quatrefoil ornamentation is
peculiar to this district and one sees it on the smallest buildings and
in the most unexpected places.

Street names are as expressive as the architecture. In Grope Lane,

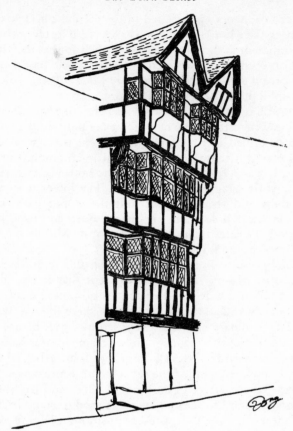

FIG 10   Tudor house, Tewkesbury, Gloucestershire

for instance, the houses overhang to such an extent that the occupants could easily reach out from the upper windows and touch their
opposite neighbours. Little daylight could penetrate into the narrow
little lane and so passers by would often have to grope their way
along.

South, in Herefordshire, the ornamentation is less lavish but the
picturesqueness remains. Ledbury is one of the most delightful of
the county's market towns with many-gabled timber-frame houses

having later tenements sandwiched in between them. The oldest of all, known as the House on Props, has jettied storeys which push their way right across the pavement—so much so that they had to be supported on crutches, ie wooden pillars on stone bases, similar to those supporting the seventeenth-century Market Hall, which stands on sixteen solid pillars of Spanish chestnut.

There are still one or two medieval timber-frame houses to be seen in towns like Worcester, some of which were built on the lines of the hall house described in Chapter Four. Where there was space and wood was plentiful these houses were fairly common, but if space was limited it was more usual to build the house of two storeys or to have the solar wing without the hall. The lower part would be used for shop and storage space and the upper part for living quarters. On the whole there are many more survivals from the Tudor period and later than there are from the Middle Ages, which virtually ended in the fifteenth century.

Tudor timber-frame building in the towns differed little from that of the previous late medieval period except that it was altogether more secular. The Church had ceased to dominate men's lives by this time. Society had advanced to a stage where life was reasonably secure and the ordinary man felt a new sense of well-being, a feeling expressed in some of the beautiful timber-frame houses he built. The Old House, Hereford (Fig 11), built by John Abel, the King's Carpenter, in the early part of the seventeenth century is a Jacobean town house that is perfect in design and detail and has fortunately been preserved for all to see and enjoy. It used to stand in Butcher's Row but it was removed to its present position in High Town when the town was developed.

Many pleasant towns, full of timber-frame buildings, grew up in Tudor times and it is interesting to trace the story of a town's rise to prosperity through its buildings. In Essex, for instance, one can trace the centres of the clothing industry through Colchester, Dedham, Coggleshall, Halstead, and Braintree. In Coggleshall there is a remarkable timber-frame house called Paycocke's, after the

---

Weatherboarding. Plate 9 (*above*) Houses at Hook Road, Epsom, Surrey; Plate 10 (*below*) plastered and weatherboarded houses at Cottered, Hertfordshire

Fig 11   Jacobean house, Hereford

wealthy cloth merchant, Thomas Paycocke, who built it for himself at the beginning of the sixteenth century. It bears a shield with a merchant's mark of an ermine's tail and the initials of Thomas Paycocke, who died in 1580. It has survived almost unaltered and has been taken into the care of the National Trust. It is regarded as pure native English Gothic without any hint of Renaissance influence. The closely spaced timbers mark it as early Tudor. The jettied upper storey projects about 18in, which is the usual overhang for this kind of house. Each storey is divided by buttresses into five bays and there are some interesting statues under canopies—a man holding a shield, and another carrying a load on his shoulder. The decorations are equally beautiful inside the house, the moulded and carved

Plate 11 (*above left*) Partially uncovered wattle and daub panels in house at Bromesberrow, Herefordshire; Plate 12 (*above right*) door with wicket, decorated frame and brick panels, Lavenham, Suffolk; Plate 13 (*below*) medieval carpenters' marks on house in Grope Lane, Shrewsbury

D

ceiling beams, original doorways, and linenfold panelling being characteristic of the period.

Houses such as this were in the 'middle' category, built in the transitional period which we call Tudor.

Lavenham, Suffolk, is typical of the many East Anglian towns that rose to prosperity in the sixteenth century. It has a fine Market Square and the best timbered Guildhall in all the county. The town is so full of genuine Tudor architecture that it is difficult to single out one building more than another; but the old Wool Hall is one of the most perfectly restored houses in Lavenham, an example of the excellent work done by the Society for the Preservation of Ancient Buildings. There are two-storeyed wings on each side of the main hall, which is entered through arched doorways with carved spandrels. A massive king-post supports the roof of the hall and the carving on the beams is among some of the best in Suffolk. But all the streets are full of delightful houses, timber-framed and plastered in the East Anglian tradition, many of them almost unaltered since the days of Elizabeth. There are close-timbered jettied houses, with ornamented timbers, some with their upper storeys leaning perilously to one side, supported by next-door neighbours (Fig 12). In between are squat plastered houses with tiny dormers in the roof, or tall thin Gothic-type houses, dignified and aloof. In fact, it is possible to see almost every kind of medieval and early Renaissance architecture in Lavenham if one looks carefully enough.

Some very delightful towns also grew up within the old Midland forest country, the Forest of Arden, where the oak was as common as the elm, and there were woods and copses as well as great heaths, yielding plenty of timber for building. That part of Warwickshire which includes Stratford-upon-Avon, Henley-in-Arden, and Alcester is particularly rich in old houses built with local materials—oak framing with wattle and daub infilling, the 'wattle' made of hazel, willow, or oak. Stratford has had its share of publicity as Shakespeare's birthplace, but it was none the less an important town before he was born in 1564.

There is an unexpected reminder of seventeenth-century London tucked away at the rear of the Borough High Street, Southwark, and almost opposite the entrance to the famous George Inn. It is known as Calvert's Buildings and has been listed as being of architectural

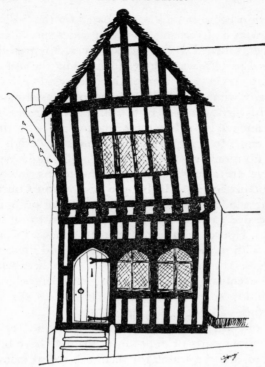

FIG 12   Medieval house, Lavenham, Suffolk

and historical interest (Grade 2) under a section of the Town and Country Planning Act. It is described as 'seventeenth century, two storey, with plaster on old timber frame and overhanging first storey'. The overhang is on the south side and there is a twin-gabled roof. Inside the house are some of the original oak beams, well preserved. The premises take their name from Calvert's, a firm of brewers, and a Felix Calvert occupied one of the buildings from 1786 to 1794; but the houses are known to be a good deal older than that.

When James I forbade the building of overhanging storeys in London because of the risk of fire, as well as for reasons of economy, the order did not apply to other towns. Nevertheless, a more

restrained design became fashionable, based on the 'balloon frame'
principle—ie with no overhang, and with wider-spaced studs reaching to the eaves, stiffened with diagonal braces. A remarkable variety
of contour and pattern was achieved simply by the use of straight
timbers and by varying the form of the oriel windows.

A later type of window, which was seen in towns around 1665–75,
is called the Ipswich window (Plate 36). It is tripartite and straight
topped, with an arch below the top of the middle light, either flat or
with bowed ends. It is a charming and unusual design, not often
seen, but by no means confined to East Anglia, as its name would
suggest. There are a few examples in the towns and villages of
Berkshire, notably in East Hagbourne and Sutton Courtenay. But
the unpopular window tax of 1695 put a restraint on building, and
to avoid excessive payments many people began to fill in some of
their windows. Houses with fewer than ten windows were taxed 2s
a year, those with more than ten windows 6s, and those with more
than twenty 10s. The tax was increased six times between 1746 and
1808 and was eventually repealed in 1851, but it left behind a trail of
bricked-in window spaces, like so many closed eyes, that can still be
seen in old houses all over the country.

There are, of course, many more timber-frame houses to be seen
in towns in various parts of the country than we have been able to
enumerate here, and the search for them can reveal many a hidden
treasure. Many of those which survive in market towns no doubt
owe their survival to the fact that the town passed its heyday many
years ago and the great commercial houses were no longer swallow-
ing up the land. This is particularly apparent in the wool towns of
East Anglia, where a peaceful seclusion descended after the decline
of the wool trade at the beginning of the last century.

FOUR

Medieval and Early Tudor

It is difficult to classify timber-frame housing by periods because so many of its traditional characteristics are rooted in the long age which we term medieval, when the church dominated the land. Broadly speaking, the medieval or Middle Ages lasted from the Dark Ages to the Reformation—from about AD 600 to 1500—and the Tudor period from 1485 to 1560, with a transitional period known as the Renaissance from 1501 to 1625, so that each new period overlapped the other and made its influence felt gradually. The technique of timber-frame building was not affected by these changes nearly as much as other methods that were rapidly coming to the fore as one period slid into the next. It was more the convenience of the building and the improvement in social conditions which made properly framed houses available to the common man.

The Black Death of 1349 was the indirect cause of a revolution in domestic building at all levels. Almost overnight the heavy mortality rate caused an acute shortage of labour, thereby doubling its market value. The farmer, left with no one to work his land, changed from arable farming to pasturage for sheep and unwittingly laid the foundation of his own future wealth and the general prosperity of the country. Within a short time the wool trade was booming and sheep farmers, weavers, and merchants became rich, many of them becoming free men for the first time in their lives. Wealth spread rapidly in the fifteenth century and there was a great social upheaval in England, followed by many changes. The new middle classes emerged with a great desire to better themselves and to build houses which would bear comparison with that of the lord of the manor, so by the first decades of the sixteenth century there were innumerable owners of houses between the wealthy nobleman and the lowly cottager.

At first, bad communications and difficulties of transport made it impossible for any but the most elaborate and costly of buildings to be built in anything but the local materials; therefore we find timber buildings largely concentrated in areas that were thickly forested, especially the West Midlands, East Anglia, Kent, and Sussex. There was also a fair amount in parts of Hertfordshire, Buckinghamshire, and Bedfordshire, and, farther to the west, in Berkshire, Hampshire, parts of Oxfordshire, Wiltshire, and Gloucestershire.

Construction was a masterpiece of local co-operation and organisation for the times. The great trees were felled and dragged to the 'framyngplace' by slow horse-drawn waggon or borne there by water—a common and fairly cheap mode of transport in the Middle Ages when England's rivers were more navigable than they are today. The wood was used green and allowed to season as work progressed, and according to old documents and accounts which list the labourers' building hours, this was at a slow and leisurely rate, so the timber had a chance to dry out during building operations. Nevertheless, oak has a great tendency to warp, which accounts for the irregular and sometimes distorted appearance of old beams, and the builders tried to overcome this problem by using massive timbers, regardless of economy. To a certain degree they were successful, and from a purely aesthetic standpoint it is this very irregularity which gives old beams their visual appeal. Our ancestors rightly believed that the smoke from the central hearth was sufficient to harden the timbers, and smoke-blackened beams are always as hard as iron.

It appears to have been the normal practice for the carpenter to cut, prepare and assemble the timbers of the frame in his own yard, marking the joints ready for assembly on site. Beams, posts, joists and so on were all mortised and tenoned while still on the ground. The heavy joints were numbered with a system of Roman numerals (Arabic numerals were unknown until the time of the Renaissance) usually made with a tool called a 'scribe' for cutting straight lines. In Jacobean times much smaller figures were used, cut with a gouge or chisel. The system was simple but effective for the craftsmen used various combinations of I, V and X which, though not strictly Latin, they were able to follow when it came to erecting the timbers and fitting the matching parts of a joint together. In their system the

Roman IV became IIII and IX became VIIII. One theory about this method is that medieval carpenters were unable to subtract, but as timbers could be turned on site it is more likely that they adopted their system because XI upside down becomes IX, which would not be correct. The number V was often cut upside down, presumably because the second stroke of the scribe working from the apex would tend to follow the first groove across the grain, therefore it would be possible for IV to become confused with VI if the timber was reversed. They also made one stroke do duty in both ten and five when used together and two or more tens shared one crossing stroke, thus saving time (see Fig 13).

IIII	Λ	ΛI	VIIII	XI	XV	XVI	XX	XXV
4	5	6	9	11	15	16	20	25

FIG 13 Medieval carpenters' numerals

A 'scribing compass' was used for making the circles and segments which were added to one of the terminal strokes of the Roman numeral (Fig 14) to denote the position of a timber, ie a side of a building, a roof truss, and so on. The frame was then dismantled and carted to the site where the timbers were sorted and erected, secured by wooden pegs firmly driven through holes made by an auger. Not a nail was used anywhere in frame assembly. In surviving medieval buildings the carpenters' marks are often still visible, particularly in the roof timbers, and they usually run in sequence, thus indicating an original structure. Close study of the marks at Shrewsbury (Plate 13)

FIG 14 Medieval carpenters' marks

show on the left number 12, in the centre number 11, and on the right another 11. The untidy appearance of the last mark and the fact that for many years their significance was forgotten leads us to think that a timber has been replaced, and noticing marks on the others the erectors have tried to copy it, incorrectly, as this should be number 10 counting the sequences on either side.

Extra help was often needed to set up the frame and this was where the neighbours lent a hand, but if the newcomer eventually proved to be a troublesome member of the community they were just as likely to pull the house down again and send him packing. It would have been a simple matter to knock out the panels and pegs and pull down the framing in the reverse order to which it had been put up.

When the house was small, according to Salzman, there is some reason to think that all the timbers of the two ends, short of the roof, would be assembled and pegged together and raised as a whole, but in larger houses the timbers would have to be raised separately. Either way, it was quite a feat, and, to judge by accounts, called for free drinks all round when it was done. Many buildings have on their heavy posts, about 6ft from the bottom, a wedge-shaped socket into which a prop was placed to support it during construction (Fig 15).

If it was not placed on the beaten earth the frame was most likely erected on a rectangular foundation of masonry or stones, to keep the oak away from the damp and to provide a level surface. First came the ground sills, consisting of great balks of timber mortised together at the corners, then the principal upright posts were mortised into the angles of the timbers and pegged loosely together for security. The tenons on the upper ends of the posts were mortised into horizontal beams called wall plates, which in turn supported the timbers of the roof. When all timbers were in position the temporary loose pegs were removed and oversize permanent pegs hammered in. In this way the basic framework of the simple single-bay dwelling was erected, but this method does not apply to crucks, which were assembled in the manner described in Chapter One.

There were two distinct types of framing up: (1) the closely set uprights divided by a transverse beam, and (2) framing in large panels (Fig 16). In the former, the uprights were at first set at intervals equal to their own width, and where there were wide spaces between studs the frame was strengthened with curved braces and diagonals, jointed and pegged to the posts. The panels were filled

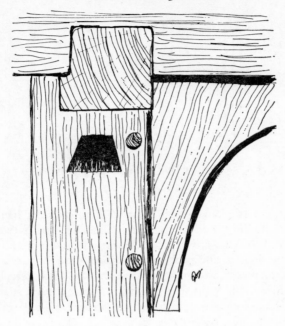

FIG 15   Socket for prop, Worcestershire

with wattle and daub, plaster, or at a later age with brick or stone, the filling varying with the district.

It is usually taken for granted that the framing of closely set studs is the earlier type but this is not always the case. It may depend on the locality and the amount of timber that was readily available, it may mean that the builder was not absolutely certain of his material and was afraid to build in the widely spaced frames that became general later, or it may even be an indication of the original owner's ability to pay for such an amount of material. There was a steep rise in the cost of timber between the fifteenth and sixteenth centuries because so much was used for iron-smelting, charcoal-burning and domestic heating, and this rise undoubtedly had its effect on the cost of building.

Both types of framing are often seen in the same locality, but,

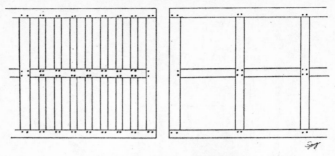

FIG 16   Close timbering and post and span

generally speaking, Worcestershire and Herefordshire have more of the wider panelling, and Shropshire, Cheshire, and Lancashire the close-set studs, with many regional variations in the methods used to preserve the timbers and in the decorations. One feature of medieval building remained fairly constant and that was the 'jetty', or over-hanging storey. The principle behind it was that each storey should be built separately—ie platform construction—with the upper storeys cantilevered over those beneath to give a wide overhang. There have been many reasons advanced for the building of the jetty. Some authorities say that the medieval carpenter did not know any other way to erect a multi-storey house, and this was the practical solution to over-springy floors caused by the practice of laying floor joists flat, instead of on edge as is now the practice. The tendency to movement was counteracted by allowing them to project beyond the wall of the storey below. The framing of the upper storey could then follow the pattern of the one beneath, the sill being laid along the ends of the projecting joists and so on, so that the weight of the building gave the floor joists the necessary stability. It was not until well on into the seventeenth century that the house wrights discovered that joists laid on their edge were much firmer and stronger and lost the tendency to whippiness. But this theory does not take into account the presence of jetties at one end of a building only, or simply a jettied gable. The overhanging storey may have been merely a device for making the upper rooms larger in an age when building land was scarce and valuable. It may have been designed as a protection for callers, but if it was for protection it was far more likely to protect the ground-floor timbers—to throw the rain water clear of them and keep them as dry as possible. It would certainly be a shelter for the goods displayed on a shop counter. There may be some truth in all these theories but in the final analysis it was undoubtedly a question of expediency and style. It was a very pleasant fashion, which gave the carpenter unending opportunities to display his skill in the fashioning of a corner post or brackets, the moulding of a fascia board, and other individual details.

FIG 17   Medieval house, Ledbury, Herefordshire

The Hall House

It is almost impossible to classify the medieval timber-frame house by regions, but there are certain local tendencies to be found in some areas. One such is the early Tudor yeomen's idea of imitating the manor house of their former masters, the great barons. The plan had the open central hall as the nucleus, flanked by two-storeyed wings at right-angles in the form of annexes, and known as the solar and service wings in true medieval tradition. The solar wing, which was

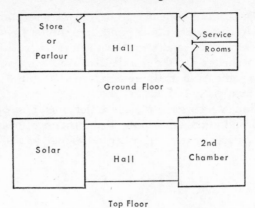

Ground Floor

Top Floor

FIG 18   Ground- and first-floor plan, medieval hall house

essentially the private dwelling of the owners, had a projecting first floor which sometimes had two rooms on it called the Great Chamber and the Ante-Chamber but more usually there was just one large room. The size of this single chamber would be increased considerably by the jettied construction, which might easily overhang some 18in beyond the framing below. To construct this chamber a great wooden girder was thrown across between the principal posts on each side of the building to take the joists, which were placed longitudinally. The floorboards, which might be as much as 3in thick, were laid on the joists without the use of nails anywhere. This was a popular method of floor construction in the Middle Ages and was tremendously weighty and strong. Where no jetty was built on the joists they were easily removable. Another method was for the joist to be mortised to a girder, but still only laid on to the horizontal timbers of the outer wall frame (see Fig 19). To provide a jetty, longer joists were used.

FIG 19   Medieval joist

According to Barley, writing in *The English Farmhouse and Cottage*, 'a possible reason for not fastening the floor boards of a chamber was that they had often been inserted by a tenant; the boards were left loose so that he could remove them if he wished. They are, like the glass of windows, not infrequently included in an inventory along with furniture. Secondly, when both joists and floor boards were loose it was much easier to get bulky goods, such as bales of wool or sacks of corn, into a chamber by removing part of the floor than by struggling up a narrow winding stair'.

In a small building of about 16ft span or less the floor joists might be carried across between the wall timbers and jointed into them, without the need for additional beams to support them, but the idea of laying on the joists without locking was the most prevalent, especially when the upper floor projected beyond the lower. Where the jetty was to be carried round all sides, as in later buildings of the period, it necessitated the use of 'dragon' or diagonal beams at an angle to the jettied floors and into which short joists were mortised to project both ways. It was an arrangement that commended itself to the Tudor carpenter and became an accepted internal feature of the four-sided jettied house, decorative or not, according to one's aesthetic tastes, for it was generally visible in the room below (Plate 22). Outside the building the dragon beam was supported by the corner post and an added supporting bracket, an obvious opportunity for further decoration (Plates 23 and 24). In some cases a tree upside down supplied the correct shape to cut post and bracket in one piece; these were called teazle posts and are found in many areas. In earlier types of building the projecting floor joists were concealed with a moulded fascia board, as at Pattyndenne Manor (see frontispiece), but this idea was abandoned in time and the ends were simply rounded off.

As in other buildings the wall spaces between the principal posts were framed with smaller upright posts, commonly called 'studs', the spaces being filled with wattle and daub panels. Windows were simply unglazed spaces, guarded from intruders by square mullions set diagonally between 3 and 6in apart, and closed with a sliding shutter rebated into the timbers attached to the beams framing the aperture (see Fig 20), rather like the modern sliding door. There was usually one large window at the end of the hall to light the master's table and a small one over the doorway to light the screens passage, for, like the manor, this house had its draught screens at the lower end of the hall.

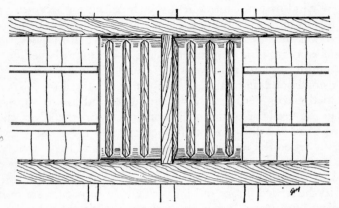

FIG 20 Medieval mullioned window with shutters

Doors were made of vertical boarding, worked into ridges and hollows to conceal the joins, framed by the ground sill with heavy oak jambs at each side and either a flat lintel at the top or an ornamental doorhead. They were often made in two halves like stable doors, to allow the top half to be opened for additional light and ventilation.

In some areas each wing was framed and roofed separately and could be removed, if need be, without damaging the hall. Or it could be enlarged equally well by framing up the extra room or storey required and adding it on piecemeal. The skeleton framework of one of these early houses looks quite complex at first sight, like a structural jigsaw puzzle, but a closer look shows clearly where additions have been made, with struts and heavy wall braces to stiffen up the timbers, and here and there a shaft of daylight through the gaps between the framing showing the division between the structures. On close inspection many a house can be seen to be a single hall unit with added wings, and it was the very flexibility of this plan that made it so suited to the needs of the 'rising' man: he could enlarge and beautify his home as his financial position improved, and succeeding generations could likewise make alterations and improvements at will.

FIG 21 Small medieval house, Halling, Kent

There are some surviving houses built to this pattern still to be seen, notably in Worcestershire, Herefordshire, and the West Midlands. Upper Brook End, Bromesberrow, is such a house. It dates back to 1424, when its original name was Hall Place. During some recent restoration work the old framework revealed the separate structures of the wings and the roof, enabling the owner to piece together a little more of the long and interesting history of a house that has had various additions over the years.

The Wealden House

A second type of yeoman's house, which was very popular with the well-to-do, is known as the Wealden house. Certain features suggest that it developed from the aisled hall in Kent, where the wealthiest yeomen were to be found, and it is a classic instance of the process of imitation, which we can trace all through medieval building.

The Wealden house has a central hall open to the roof, with a projecting wing at one end or both, but the whole built under a continuous roof and framed as one unit. The external wall of the central hall is recessed, the roof being supported by curved braces fixed under the eaves plate and extending to the wings (Fig 23). There is nearly always a cross passage, though if the hall is particularly small this may be in the service wing. There is a good example of this type of house at Alfriston, Sussex—a fourteenth-century priest's house. It has two rooms at the eastern end, corresponding to the medieval retiring room and solar, and a further two at the western end, divided by the central hall, where there is some beautiful timbering to be seen. Fragments of the carving, which was done 600 years ago, are still visible on the beams of the open roof; and there are some interesting contrasting doors, two with depressed ogival heads from the hall to the service rooms, now converted to one room, and another exterior door in the hall with an equilateral head. This property was the first purchased by the National Trust and has been restored nearly to its original form.

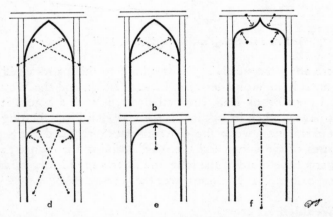

FIG 22 Door heads: (a) lancet, (b) equilateral, (c) ogee, (d) four-centred, (e) semi-circular, (f) segmental

There is another example of this type of yeoman's house at Bignor, Sussex, built about the mid-fifteenth century. It has a pair of curved braces supporting the thatched roof under the recessed portion,

where there are also four herring-bone brick panels, probably put in to replace a bay window when an upper floor was inserted during the sixteenth century, or after. It has various panels filled with brick or flint over the years as the wattle and daub has collapsed. The house is built on stone foundations, and has so many courses above ground that it needs half a dozen brick steps to reach the door. For part of its life it was the village grocer's shop and still has its extra door. It is referred to locally as The Old Shop, though it has long since been a private house. Because it has been altered so little over the centuries it is possible to see clearly all the facets and features of the original Wealden house.

FIG 23   Wealden House, Bignor, Sussex

It is in fact the only specialised or regional type of timber-framing in south-east England. In Kent, all the traditional English building materials were available, so it was natural that the great oak forests that once covered the Weald were used extensively for these hall houses. They are to be seen throughout the Weald of Sussex and

---

Traditional types of roofing. Plate 16 (*above left*) Thatcher dressing Norfolk reed thatch on house in Hampshire; Plate 17 (*above right*) heavy stone roof at Welshpool, Montgomeryshire; Plate 18 (*below left*) 250-year-old oak shingles, Horsmonden, Kent; Plate 19 (*below right*) rare wattle support found under old straw thatch at Quarley, Hampshire

E

Kent, where the clothing industry and iron smelting brought prosperity.

Two in Otham are especially interesting—Ward's, dating from the time of Edward III and built on the L plan, and Synyards, built in the latter half of the fifteenth century and typical of its period and style (Plate 7).

It has been suggested that Kent became the home of large numbers of well-to-do yeomen because of the security of tenure offered by the local system of inheritance, 'gavelkind', whereby the lands of a person dying intestate descended to his sons and daughters in equal shares. Such protection was a great inducement to the moderately wealthy man to settle in the county and may well be the basis of its proverbial prosperity.

But the type of house which evolved from the Kentish yeoman's way of life was not necessarily confined to Kent, though that is where it is most likely to be found today. It is to be seen in the south-eastern counties and as far afield as the West Midlands and the North, in diminishing numbers. This probably means that the medieval carpenters who built to this plan travelled around in the course of their work—perhaps on some large building project—and took their ideas with them. These ideas in later years were subjected to regional variations. Some houses give us a clue to the original standing of their owners by the quality of their finish, ie moulded ceiling beams and braces, the buttress-like projection of a main post, as at Pattyndenne, the insertion of an oriel window, perhaps with the lights rising to a traceried head, a good fireplace, and a dozen other details which proclaim a 'manor house' status. Others, with rougher finish to the beams, or a simple ladder instead of a spiral stair, indicate a sturdy yeoman origin.

On the whole, this was an inexpensive type of house to build, another reason for its general popularity, and it was well into the seventeenth century before the plan was abandoned. So the houses that are left to us from the Middle Ages are mostly yeomen's houses, for there were no cottages as we know them before about 1550, and even then the word 'cottage' has been so misused that descriptions are apt to be confusing. What seemed to matter more than the size of a house was the amount of land that went with it. The literal meaning of the term 'yeoman' is a small landowner, especially a freeholder holding free land of 40s value; though what we know as a yeoman's house may well have belonged to a master weaver, a tanner, a glover, ironmaster or miller, or indeed a house wright who became a successful man and could well afford to own land. It was also primarily a farmer's house, based on his concept of a medieval manor house. The favourite design for the farmhouse was an L shape, with a range of buildings divided into hall and cross passage with an additional wing for service. The arm of the L was used for storing grain and other products and additions could be made by framing up another bay and building on as and when it was needed. The carpenters were becoming increasingly successful in making timber-frame houses more convenient for their users. Sometimes a date carved on a gable with the initials of a former owner will reveal the time when an alteration or addition was made. At Moat Farm, Dormston, Worcestershire, the date 1663 and the initials T.C. are carved on a stone plaque on a gable; but even without a close examination of the interior construction, it is quite obvious from the exterior timbers that the house was built at least a century before that (Plate 6).

Most of the large farmhouses in East Anglia were built on the H pattern, the centre block having once been the open hall. Generally, they are unostentatious in design, often plastered in the regional style, with some pargeting to relieve the surface.

The early Tudor farmer built his house in the village, or township, away from the holdings, which were distributed piecemeal among the common fields; and it was not until enclosure began that he built his farmhouse on his own land. But it must be borne in mind that enclosure had been proceeding slowly since the fifteenth century by a number of Acts and was not really complete until the eighteenth century, the rate of enclosure of acres varying with the county. This accounts for the disposition of farmhouses about the countryside and the comparatively isolated units of buildings still having the feudal effect.

The Small House

William Harrison, a sixteenth-century Essex parson wrote: 'In times past men were content to dwell in houses built of sallow, willow, plumtree, hardbeam and elm, so that the use of oak was almost

wholly for churches, nobleman's lodgings and navigation.' But in
the mid-sixteenth century it became possible for the first time for all
but the very poorest to build a lasting house for himself. It was a
golden age for the house carpenter. The people demanded oak,
formerly the privilege of the lord for his manor or the monk for his
abbey, and the small houses began to go up apace.

It appears to have been accepted that if a builder could get his
frame erected and the ridge piece fixed between dusk and dawn the
structure was regarded as an accomplished fact. So it came about
that many a labourer's cottage was hastily planted by night on the
common land. Some of these opportunists would probably already
possess 'squatter's rights' on land which they had previously cleared
from the forests; others would have rights of pasture and common,
which entitled them to any small timber and fuel they could gather
and also allowed them to keep a beast.

These little houses were generally constructed by the post and
truss method, which superseded the cruck in most areas, though the
latter method would still be used in conservative localities, and if
suitable timbers were available. Either way, the roof was steep, and,
on the newer type of house, either hipped or gable ended, unbroken
as yet by dormers; and the building was seldom more than one room
in span, that one room sometimes making up the whole house. One
up and one down constituted the extent of the house if it was
storeyed (few small ones *were* originally) and the whole structure
would measure only about 23ft long and 16–18ft wide. The plan was
simple, consisting of a ground-floor living-room and kitchen combined, with a ladder-like stairway leading directly into the room
above. Some houses followed the 'long house' plan, with two rooms
open to the roof side by side. The characteristic overhang of the
storeyed house, so typically Tudor, combined with the steep roof,
often of heavy thatch, gave these little houses a top-heavy look.

Windows were small and in some places set high up in the wall,
particularly in Essex, where they are immediately under the eaves in
the upper storey and at ceiling level on the ground floor. If the
intention was to keep the draughts out one wonders how successful
they were. They allowed a better dispersion of light, and this may
have been their purpose; or, more likely, it was convenient to use the
wall plate or other beam for the top of the window.

The Tudor period was characterised by the diamond-paned lattice in domestic buildings. It was a reminder of the early methods of filling in the 'wind hole' with a lattice of withies woven diagonally to allow the rain water to drain downwards. Now, the small diamond-shaped panes were joined together by lead strips and lights separated by moulded mullions. Their number grew less with each storey, which served to emphasise the superior importance of the ground-floor room, or living-room. The openings between the mullions by now averaged about 15in wide and might vary between 2 and 3ft in height, according to the size of the house.

The doorway, which led straight into the living-room, was made up of stout boards, set edge to edge, with two cross battens and a diagonal between to keep them firm. They were fastened together with oak pegs or imitation nails and the door was locked from the inside by a long bar slid into position. A wooden sneck latch, operated by a piece of string threaded through a hole to the outside of the door, was a rudimentary method of opening and shutting the door, and it is still in use today.

The earliest type of flooring for the ground floor was just beaten earth strewn with rushes. Upstairs, wide boards of oak or elm on joists were used. Now, polished smooth with the wear of centuries and often with a decided slope in one direction where the house has settled on its earth foundations, these old floorboards are still a beautiful feature of many a restored cottage. Brick and quarry floors are a later innovation.

In general the basic construction of these little houses did not vary a great deal. They differed mostly in the finishing and, regionally, in the number and dispersion of rooms. Occasionally elm would be used for some of the interior beams instead of oak, and though it was rougher it was never unpleasing. The people were proud of their oak beams, and the touches of decorative craftsmanship—a circle in the panel of the framing, maybe, or a cusp, fashioned out of a crooked piece of timber that was useless for other purposes. Whatever it was, it was the outward symbol of the personal freedom of some rural worker or smallholder in those early post-feudal days.

There are few original early Tudor cottage homes left today; although there are some in the vernacular Tudor style in Kent and some weavers' cottages in Suffolk, the survivors are mostly from a later period. If we are fortunate enough to find the remnants of an early one it is nearly always as the nucleus of a larger house. It is only by tracing the timbers back to their beginnings by means of the joiners' marks that we can sometimes unravel the history of a house, and this can be a most rewarding exercise.

Even less often do we come across a detached cottage of this period; they are more usually found in a row. There are some good examples of cottage rows at Ombersley in Worcestershire and at Wherwell in Hampshire. Another at Chiddingstone, Kent, is preserved by the National Trust. Very often a closer look will reveal that the supposed row was once a farmhouse, now converted into two or three cottages, the long line of the roof and the central chimney stack giving a clue to its origin. Or it may even be a long house with additions.

Usually it is difficult to tell the date of the original building without access to some old records or wills. In the Middle Ages it was almost a compulsory duty for a man to make an inventory of his goods for taxation purposes, and to make a will to which the Church usually acted as executor. Wills and inventories, therefore, are very detailed and give us a fascinating insight into a man's life and property in those far off days.

FIVE

The Plan Simplified

The long reign of Elizabeth (1558–1603) marked the passing of the main features of the Middle Ages and the birth of modern England. It was an exciting age, when a new spirit of enterprise and adventure was making itself felt in trade as well as in politics. Towards its close timber began to get scarce and more expensive. The price had risen by as much as 25 per cent in a few years and the economists were seriously alarmed. There had been heavy demands for shipbuilding—the Queen was building up a huge fleet of ships—and for fuel, as well as for the great numbers of houses that had gone up in all the timber-building areas in the past few decades; so there was a call for new economies and a cutting down on the amount of timber used for new buildings. The jetty construction was considered wasteful and out of date and it became the practice to build the frame in one piece from ground to eaves, a construction called the 'balloon frame'.

The style of building began to change under the influence of the Italian Renaissance and its emphasis on classic simplicity. It affected timber-frame building by its insistence on a more symmetrical design, as opposed to the straggling appearance of medieval days.

Even smaller houses, which were not unduly affected by Continental influence, made some attempt at symmetry in planning, with gables and bays in harmony with each other, additional rooms provided, and more lighting through bigger windows. The desire for more comfort and privacy was the major factor in house design in this transitional period. The Renaissance effect was seen in timber building in the design of doorways and windows, where starkly simple square heads with label moulds took the place of the lovely Tudor arch that had dominated the façade for so long. But if the exterior was made more orderly, the interior was as decorative as ever, with every evidence of the craftsman's skill and pride in his work, for people were much more wealthy than in a previous age. Those who had been content with houses of three to five rooms now wanted six or nine rooms, and they were willing to pay the price for good workmanship and lavish decoration. A large house still had its ranks of soaring gables and beautifully carved barge boards, but the old impression of 'bittiness' was gone. The simplified plan saved timber. In general the balloon frame had become standard building practice by the beginning of the seventeenth century and has lasted ever since.

Fig 24　Rowley's House, Shrewsbury, Shropshire

As the shortage of home-grown timber increased it became necessary to import wood from Scandinavia. This was softwood, easier to work than our tough native oak and with less tendency to warp, but much weaker in its load-bearing capacity. However, it had been discovered by this time that floor joists laid on their edge were able to bear far greater loads than those laid on their sides, so from this time onwards it became customary to lay these imported 'deals' edge-wise, in modern fashion, and to conceal them with a lath and plaster ceiling below. The oak-beamed effect was on the way out and with it went some of the natural beauty and individual character of timber-frame building.

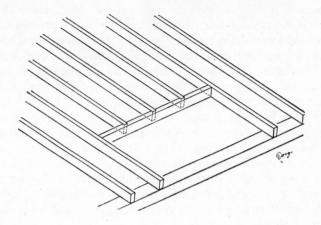

FIG 25 Joists laid on edge and trimmed

In the interests of economy smaller timbers were used, and massive oak beams and 'summers' in all their rugged native beauty became a thing of the past.

Cottages and Small Houses

The reign of Elizabeth was an important period in the development of the English village, which soon became a thriving self-contained community. But there were two big interrelated problems at this transitional stage, which had to be met with careful legislation. The first was the great increase in population, which had risen from 2,500,000 at the beginning of the fifteenth century to 6,500,000 by the end of the sixteenth, and the consequent need to increase food production. The second was the tremendous spate of cottage building, which had gone on unchecked since about 1550 and now threatened to get out of hand.

To meet the first need the authorities restricted the extent of pasturage and insisted on tillage of the land sufficient for the wants of the community, in direct reversal of the policy which had followed in the wake of the Black Death. Then, by a Statute of 1589, new cottage building was discouraged, presumably to prevent the flood of 'squatters' from pasturing on the land and becoming a potential burden on the rates. Some of these were probably people who had been evicted from their cottages in other villages or who had been forced to surrender their holdings as the fields were enclosed. This Act of Elizabeth's 'against the creating and maintaining of cottages' also refers to the 'erecting of great numbers of cottages, which are daily more and more increased in many parts of this Realm'. In a way it was a wise law, for it laid down that 4 acres of land should be attached to each cottage let to agricultural labourers and no cottage was to be occupied by more than one family. The rule exempted seafaring folk, tradesmen, and craftsmen, which accounts for many artisan cottages which sprang up outside agricultural communities and near rivers. Wind-powered or water-powered mills, equipped with immensely strong wooden machinery, provided work for great numbers of people.

Towards the end of the sixteenth century, Harrison tells us, the situation was greatly improved. Unemployment had practically disappeared and the specialist craftsman and tradesman were more numerous than ever before, well able to meet the demands of those who were now 'house conscious'. The tiler, thatcher, mason, dauber, carpenter, and others were valuable members of the community and their cottages reflected their status. There is a surprising richness about some of these little houses, which shows perhaps in the foliations of a barge board, the charm of an oriel window, or an elaborately carved post. The districts which grew rich through trade in Elizabethan days can easily be identified by the standard of their housing, much of which, happily, still survives in the timber-building areas. The villages of East Anglia, for instance, where almost every cottage had a loom and shared in the general prosperity of the cloth trade; or the Midlands, where the great ironmasters, potters, glassmakers, or tanners created work for thousands; were much more prosperous than the north of England, for instance, which was generally reckoned to be a century behind the south-east in development.

The small cottage did not change much at this time. If it can be said to have had a 'plan', it existed in the mind of the house wright, who built what his client wanted, using either the modified hall or long house plans (see Fig 26).

Where the new style of building was adopted uprights were spaced wider apart and horizontal timbers divided the framework into square panels, about 3–4ft square, with diagonal braces at intervals to stiffen up the structure. Sometimes not even these diagonals were

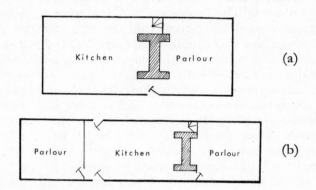

FIG 26   Ground-floor plans, Elizabethan and Jacobean

used and the result was a box-like structure with square unadorned panels set with almost mechanical precision, with one square filled by each of the windows and two by the doors (see Plate 21). This was typical of a cottage or small house, especially in the Midlands. It was plain to the point of austerity in comparison with the exuberance of medieval days, though, of course, there were always exceptions.

The rural carpenter stuck to traditional materials and methods long after they had been abandoned in the cities. If James I had forbidden the building of overhanging storeys in London because of the risk of fire, it mattered little to the country house wright whose client wanted a jettied house. In some out of the way parts he may not even have heard of the new-fangled ways, or did not want to hear of them. He was nothing if not adaptable and was quite ready to evolve his own plan of building to suit the requirements of his client, so we see the medieval house evolve into all sorts of odd combinations in different regions long after the age had faded into history. In many rural areas the cruck survived as the best means of building a range of single-storey buildings, yet the resourceful carpenter was not above building on a framed storied wing if he was asked for it. A house of this kind is to be seen at Steventon, Berkshire, where the cruck in the end wall shows its origin, and a gabled cross-wing with unusual cross-bracing is seen at the opposite end as a later addition. In this same village are some clusters of old timber-frame houses in The Causeway: Nos 103–7 are a mixture of late fourteenth century and seventeenth century, with two projecting gable wings; Nos 77–81 are also part fourteenth and part seventeenth century, with a striking feature in a great chimney breast to the street and some beautiful fretwork barge boards on the gables.

Records suggest that additional building reached its peak between 1580 and 1630 and this must have included new buildings as well as conversions of barns into cottages. This was the time when many thousands of weavers, dyers, etc, left Flanders to settle in England, mainly in the eastern counties where they could be sure of getting a living. East Anglia was never much involved in the long drawn out wars of the fifteenth century, which left the harbours of Essex, Suffolk, and King's Lynn in Norfolk relatively free for trade; and both bricks and skilled Continental craftsmen came through these ports unhindered, with the result that the workers settled in East Anglia and soon made their influence felt in the style of their building. For this reason Flemish house features, such as 'crow-stepped' gables or chimney stacks, are more widespread in East Anglia than anywhere else. Some of these attractive features are very noticeable in the districts around Lavenham and Kersey in Suffolk, where the textile trade flourished, and in the maltings and factories around Dedham.

At the beginning of the Elizabethan period the tendency was for the improvement of existing buildings rather than rebuilding, and many a cottage had a framed lean-to added at the side or a backhouse by way of extension (the equal of the yeoman's service room). Windows were made to open, and these were now in the shape of hand-wrought iron casements made by the blacksmith and hung on hooks to the frame, which was set in the framework of the house and fastened with ornamental fasteners. Bricks replaced the old earth floors in cottages and in many other ways the humble house owner reflected the growing desire for more comfort and convenience which was felt by all classes at this time.

Still later, in the eighteenth century, the flight of stairs beside the fireplace was cased in and became in fact the 'staircase', set in a cupboard with a little wooden door. It was often the only cupboard the cottage possessed, for floor space was limited, but the fashion of using corner cupboards and great oak chests for storing linen and clothes more than made up for the deficiency of built-in cupboards.

The single-span building, which had been so prominent in medieval days, was a long time dying out. It lasted until the eighteenth century, through a development of the 'long house', with rooms going right across from side to side and entered one from the other. Sometimes it was a 'two parlour' house (see Fig 26[b]), and the addition of a byre or stable at one end was often an integral part of the plan—a common sight in Hampshire single-span houses to this day (see Fig 41). The extensions were only to eaves' level and the roof was hipped, losing the typical medieval gabled end (Fig 27). There might be a variation between one and a half and two storeys, with attics or garrets giving good head room. Part of the roof space may have been given a ceiling at the level of the rafter collars (see Plate 25) to make a more comfortable chamber. In short, there are so many adaptations, all typical of the resourcefulness of the village carpenter, that it is impossible to classify them. Hertfordshire is one of the counties where the timber-frame tradition persisted well into the eighteenth century, and here and there some examples have been preserved.

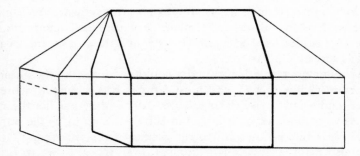

FIG 27 Fifteenth–sixteenth-century single-bay house with seven-teenth-century hipped ends

The Yeoman's House

The middle-class yeoman had his open hall divided to make a second storey, and the ceiling was supported by substantial beams. It was not long before the 'hall' was called a kitchen and the beams held great bacon racks. A framed staircase to the wings took the place of the former ladders and for the first time this staircase was made, as we know it, of treads, risers, and strings, with balusters and hand rail (see Fig 9). A house of middling size sometimes had a wing built at the rear to take such a staircase. This was the only solution if there was not a fair-sized hall or a superfluous cross passage to take it, for either a dog-leg or well-type stair took up considerably more room than the old spiral type.

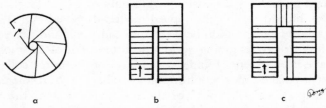

a   b   c

FIG 28   Staircase: (a) newel, (b) dog-leg, (c) well

The wastage of the space in the roof became more obvious as time progressed, and the attic storey came into use. In the small house the attics were lit by dormers cut in the roof timbers and fitted with a window frame of small lights. It was an arrangement which gave more head room and was convenient. Larger houses were provided with huge gables, as at Synyards (Plate 7) and the attics were usually used as servants' bedrooms.

In the main a farmer's prosperity could be judged by the number of service rooms he had; and most farmers had a buttery, a brew-house, and a milkhouse (later called a dairy). Many medieval farmhouses were modified or enlarged in Elizabeth's reign, as the transitional ideas filtered through to the country from the town. There were also many adaptations to houses of all types, either to bring them up to date or to give them a longer lease of life. Thus, where the timbers of the ground-floor storey had decayed—perhaps through damp—the jettied wings were henceforth supported by brick walls, or new timber-framing, so that both overhangs and recesses disappeared. With the upper walls of wood supported in this way, the occupiers could then cut holes in the floor and make fireplaces. Some old close-timbered cottages in Bridgnorth, Shropshire, show how this kind of treatment was carried out; and soon hundreds of small houses had been treated in similar fashion, but there were also hundreds of new two-roomed cottages by the end of Elizabeth's reign.

Timber was still plentiful enough to be used generously and in great variety in the West Midlands and the Welsh border counties, where the buildings assumed very distinctive regional characteristics, notably in Warwickshire, Worcestershire, Herefordshire, Shropshire, and Cheshire. The familiar black and white 'magpie' effect, with elaborate patterning on the larger houses (though not on cottages) fits in well with the landscape and adds to the scenic charm. Carpenter seems to be too mundane a title for those men who displayed sheer genius at their craft. One such was John Abel (1577–1674), whom Charles I appointed 'King's Carpenter'. He was a native of Hereford and his mastery of his art soon became apparent in the splendid building styles he perfected. He was best known for such public buildings as the Market Halls at Ledbury and at Leominster, the Old House, Hereford (see Fig 11), and the destroyed Town Hall; but the stamp of his genius can be seen in farmhouse and cottage alike, for their survival is due to sound construction with the finest of local materials. Indeed, Shropshire and Herefordshire have given us some of the finest master builders England has ever produced.

In the years before the outbreak of the Civil War (1642) the pace of building slackened and the new houses that were built were on the large side, more for the gentry than the small man, who was not so prosperous as before. As enclosures proceeded slowly and relentlessly common land and pasture gradually disappeared, with the result that more and more families moved into towns or villages to obtain work, and once again the gap between rich and poor widened. Inevitably, the war brought about a great break with the past and timber-frame building again suffered from the scarcity of materials as well as the increasing cost. Smaller timbers came to be used, often concealed behind a sheathing of lath and plaster, or the entire balloon frame might be encased in brick or stone. A timber frame beneath a plaster wall is very difficult to detect, but a thickening at the tops of the tall corner posts and a slight projection at roof level betrays it to the keen observer.

As the building trade expanded, brick or stone building became more common, and the art of building finally passed from the carpenter to the bricklayer and the mason. There was promise of the better domestic planning that was to come, in some of the timber houses that were built at this time, and in many ways the simplification of design and toning down of colour and decoration had the effect of showing off the natural beauty of timber to its best advantage.

Weatherboarding

In some south-eastern counties, particularly in coastal areas, it became the practice for builders to cover the framework of their houses externally with horizontal boarding when the original wattle and daub was no longer weatherproof. The boarding overlapped, as in shipbuilding, and was coated with pitch to protect the frame from driving rain and spray. It was known as weatherboarding, or clapboarding. It is a common type of cladding in Wales, where it often covers square framing and wattle and daub infilling. This idea was adopted by others for new buildings, using softwood boarding, especially in Kent and Sussex, where it was painted white. There is an interesting row of white, partially weatherboarded, cottages at Goudhurst, Kent (Plate 29), built in the early seventeenth century to accommodate weavers, as were many of the timbered cottages of this period in Kent. The villages of Marden, Biddenden, Lamberhurst, and others have many of these cottages, all with one main feature—a chamber large enough to take a loom. They are solidly built and look as though they may last as many more centuries as they have already stood, are pleasant to look at, and fit comfortably into the landscape of hop fields and orchards for which Kent is noted.

It followed as a natural development that a century later, during

Plate 20 (*above*) Seventeenth-century iron fireback in Tudor fireplace in house in Kent; Plate 21 (*below*) modern Western red cedar shingles on sixteenth-century house at Spetchley Common, Worcestershire

the time of the Regency (c 1815), the same kind of house should be built with a softwood frame clad in weatherboarding. The technique of softwood framing is rather different from that of oak framing, the studs being placed closer together in order to take the external boarding and the interior skin of lath and plaster. The studs are strengthened at the angles by braces and there is no infilling. Joints, too, are simpler, being simply halved, lapped and nailed. The boarding strengthened the frame in the same way as it does in a modern house. It was a cheap and economical way of building in timber and large numbers of these houses appeared in the south-east of England. Many of them, indeed, built to the new square plan with central passage and staircase, carried on the timber tradition well into the nineteenth century, particularly in the south of England. There are some good examples at Hook Road, Epsom, Surrey (Plate 9); they were built early in the nineteenth century as labourers' cottages, and in the course of time the land was taken over by the local Gas Company, now part of the South Eastern Gas Board, who keep the little white-painted houses in an excellent state of preservation.

Most houses of this type were used as cottages for workers, but it was not long before their usefulness and economy of construction were recognised, with the result that many similar weatherboarded buildings were designed for agricultural and industrial use. It was an architectural style that was introduced into some of the states of North America by English colonists, and there it reached far more splendid proportions than it ever did in its native land—in the well-known, rather stately, 'Colonial' houses that are such a fine feature of the North American countryside today.

Unfortunately, the nineteenth century cheapened the tradition of timber building in this country by shoddy imitations and an abortive attempt at reviving 'olde worlde' romance, and so there was a reaction against it. Nevertheless, some British architects and builders believed in timber as a lasting and practical building material and they were helped and encouraged by their contemporaries in America

---

Plate 22 (*above*) The dragon beam in 'Bayleaf' which was removed from Bough Beech, Kent; Plate 23 (*below left*) the corner bracket that supported it; Plate 24 (*below right*) decorated corner bracket at Lavenham, Suffolk

F

and Scandinavia, where timber building had been continuous. So a few more rural cottages were weatherboarded and plastered internally. Some were built as part of a local council housing scheme at Bucklebury, Berkshire, and it is enlightening to note that a four-roomed cottage at Merrow Common, Surrey, with storage space, built on a brick foundation with rebated boarding stained with dark brown preservative over timber framing, cost £107 in 1914. It is as good today as when it was built and fits into its wooded setting perfectly.

So this period of weatherboarding came to an end. The old timber-frame tradition was already dead, killed by the machine age and the demands of a new high-speed generation, but a new idiom was coming into being which was destined to bring timber to the fore again. This development is dealt with in Chapter Twelve.

SIX

Fireplaces and Chimneys

From the earliest days of the Anglo-Saxons, when houses were nothing but rough wooden sheds, there has been a special place for a fire. Then it was the bare earth floor, or at best a great slab of stone, on which wood, charcoal, or turf was burnt, the smoke escaping where it might—through the thatch or out of the 'wind hole' cut in the boarding of the wooden wall—for there was no chimney. That it was sooty there can be no doubt. Chaucer, in 'The Tale of the Nun's Priest', says: 'Fful sooty was hir bour and eke hire halle'. He was describing a widow's two-room house and the 'sooty bower' was the chamber in which she slept with her 'daughters two' while the servants shared the hall with the beasts, which was the normal procedure.

In the halls of the aristocracy the servants ate and slept round the fire while their lord occupied the raised dais at the end, so that, in a crude and primitive way, all shared the warmth. This central hearth in the common hall was the only means of heating, apart from braziers, and there is little historical evidence on their use.

If the hall was of any size the hearth would be made up of more than one huge slab of stone and great billet bars would be used to support the roaring log fire, the smoke escaping through an open vent, or louvre, in the form of a turret set in the high open roof. If there was no such outlet, the smoke had to find its way out through the unglazed windows or the doors, blackening the walls meantime and ruining many a priceless tapestry. Many houses and cottages still have their roof timbers coated with hard deposits of soot several hundred years old, evidence of their earlier chimneyless origin.

Understandably, a louvre was soon considered a necessity, and while it was a decorative and somewhat imposing feature on the roof of the medieval great hall, it assumed a more humble aspect on the smaller house. Mr L. F. Salzman, in his book *Building in England Down to 1540*, tells of an invoice for 'ij smoke holys' made in one William Osborne's house in Bath in 1420, at the cost of 3½d. He also describes a simple way of making a louvre by using a barrel with the ends knocked out, and quotes: '4d. paid for a cask for a louver at Cambridge in 1415'.

Sheer necessity, urged on by burning throats and streaming eyes, drove our forefathers to inventing these makeshift appliances, which no doubt helped to draw the smoke away from the house. The louvre in a turret still survives in some old timber-frame manor houses and there is a particularly good one on Milstead Manor, Kent. If it is no longer used for ventilation it may house a clock or have some other practical purpose. It often looks far too ornamental to dispense with entirely, and its true use is so obscured that many are explained away as towers for the bell that once called labourers from the field.

By the twelfth century the hall of the manor had a permanent hearth close to the upper end to warm the building, while the cooking fire was relegated to a separate kitchen connected to the hall by a covered way. Some time later, during the fourteenth century—the Early English period—it was realised that it was, in some cases, more convenient to place the hearth against a wall protected by a stone reredos or fireback. At first such hearths were used only in the withdrawing room, with a projecting hood that tapered upwards and backwards to cover a rudimentary flue taking the smoke to a vent hole or some kind of smoke chamber in the roof. In very large houses this sloping hood was made of stone, an idea which was copied to some extent in large timber-frame houses and by the use of wattle and daub smoke shafts in humbler dwellings. The smoke still had to pass out through the roof as it obviously could not pass up within the thickness of a panelled wall. Small houses and cottages that retained a central fire also copied this idea by placing a hood over the fire and moving the whole slightly towards the end gable to provide a fixing point.

With such primitive constructions the fire risk must have been considerable and it was doubly dangerous in cities. It is not surprising to find regulations in the City of London in the fourteenth century which forbade the placing of any reredos where a fire was made for cooking near partition walls of laths or boards or elsewhere where there was danger of fire. Chimneys in future were to be made of stone, tiles, or brick, and not of plaster or wood 'under pain of being pulled down'. In the Middle Ages the term chimney nearly always meant the whole fireplace; the chimney stack, as we know it, appeared later.

By the fifteenth century the wall fireplace had been introduced into the great lofty halls of the manor to replace central hearths, and by the Tudor period, with the accent on domestic building, there were many improvements: (1) through the use of a new material, brick, and (2) through the introduction of the chimney stack, both of which revolutionised fireplace design. The wholesale use of the chimney stack was due to the increased use of the new fuel, coal, which produced such an appalling smoke, far more deadly than wood smoke, that it had to be taken right away from the house. House owners who burnt wood found a chimney stack cut out a large part of the smoke problem. New buildings could have a stack incorporated in the wall, with the flue rising vertically through the stack.

When the open central fire was finally abolished it became possible to put a ceiling across the upper part of the hall, thus halving its height and conserving the warmth, as well as providing a second and even a third storey. So great two-storeyed stacks were built, to take fireplaces for the hall and the chamber above it. By placing the stack away from a wall it was possible to divide the hall into two parts horizontally as well as vertically, if desired, thereby producing four small cosy rooms in the space occupied by the great draughty hall. The massive brick structure was admirably suited to supporting the stout beams required to carry the first- and second-floor joists.

Houses of traditional late medieval design placed the hall fireplace with its back to the cross passage, or screens passage, and the fireplace itself became a huge cavernous recess, dominating the whole wall. In early days it had a massive mantel beam, hewn from good English oak, sometimes chamfered, sometimes squared off, with the marks of the adze left on. This treatment has always seemed so right for this rugged hole-in-the-wall fireplace that nothing has ever satisfactorily replaced it. Later, however, it sometimes had a four-centred stone arch over it with some form of carved decoration in the spandrels. It was often framed in stone and lined with stone or brick, sometimes with herring-bone pattern brickwork, with great fire-dogs to keep the big logs from rolling out into the room.

It was a splendid, if somewhat rugged, feature, soon to be singled out for special treatment. In the houses of the wealthy its importance was emphasised by decoration in the form of an overmantel embellished with a coat of arms—some shields or floral emblems skilfully carved in stone, wood, or brick, according to the owner's taste. In time this overmantel became a towering 'chimney piece', framing the wide hearth and rising above it to ceiling height. It was panelled and richly carved, and became a dramatic focal point of interest on which sculptors, wood-carvers and artists lavished their skill. It was, in effect, the centre of applied art in any important room.

During the Elizabethan Renaissance the designs of the Flemish and German immigrants tended to be too ornate and too richly embellished for English tastes, and though their chimney pieces in carved wood were elaborate they were not always beautiful. Many of them were wildly extravagant, with an incompatible mixture of Gothic and Renaissance ideas. But this influx of foreign craftsmen did have the effect of stimulating English workers to develop and improve their own designs, resulting in the more restrained taste of the late Renaissance period. Nevertheless, all this heavy ornamentation was only to be seen in the great houses, where there was endless competition among the owners to outdo each other in splendour and display. The smaller timber-frame manor and the unpretentious yeoman's house never aspired to such flamboyance.

The open hearth was designed solely for the burning of logs, which were perched on andirons or fire-dogs, and the fire was never allowed to go out. When we consider the tons of wood these fireplaces must have consumed, we get some idea of the alarming rate at which the country's timber was burnt up. Metal firebacks soon became a necessary protection for the stone and brickwork inside the fireplace against the fierce heat, and as coal came into more general use they became even more necessary. In the late sixteenth century many beautiful iron firebacks were made (mainly in Sussex and the neighbouring iron-founding counties) by casting molten iron in a sand mould, the design being hand-sculpted in the sand before pouring. Many of the patterns were very beautiful and quite elaborate, and it was not unusual to see a nobleman's coat of arms on his fireback, complete with heraldic devices. Simpler designs would perhaps be a Tudor rose, or the owner's initials and the date; such firebacks are so rare nowadays that they have virtually become collectors' pieces. There is a plain one in the Great Hall of Synyards at Otham, which has the date 1699 on it, with no other ornamentation. It was bought from an old inn, but that makes it no less valuable as a genuine piece of seventeenth-century craftsmanship (see Plate 20).

By the second half of the seventeenth century coal-burning became general and new grates were designed to take the fuel. They were usually basket-shaped, raised up on four legs, and were very attractive and neatly made. With the decorated iron fireback to complete the assembly of ironwork the grate lost nothing of its former interest. The design of the fireplace in general reflected the Renaissance influence, the opening being square headed and the whole surrounded by a moulded frame. In the big house the elaborate overmantel of the Elizabethan age was replaced by a simple square panel in a moulded frame, occasionally with some carved decoration within the frame; but the design was less flamboyant than its predecessor.

The situation was now ripe for a tax on hearths; Charles II was responsible for its introduction in 1662 and it was voted to the crown for ever. It was one of the most unpopular taxes ever levied. With the exception of small cottages all houses were charged at the rate of 2s for every hearth, fire, or stove, and the tax yielded £200,000 a year. It did not greatly affect the wealthy, but it was a heavy imposition on small house owners. Consequently, when William III was on his journey from Torbay and had not even reached London, scores of his new subjects begged him to relieve them of this burden. Realising that it 'was very grievous to the people' William abolished the tax, and it was eventually repealed after it had been in existence for well over a quarter of a century.

Farmhouses and Cottages
From earliest times the central fire in the homes of the yeoman farmer and the peasant was used for cooking as well as heating.

When the wattle smoke shaft came into general use it must have helped to draw up cooking smells as well as smoke. Occasionally traces of these wattle shafts are found during alterations to a timber-frame house. One such discovery was made at Hunter's Cottage, Houghton, Hampshire, where wood ash 3ft deep was found under the wooden floorboards in the living-room, pointing to the fact that there was once a central fire there. Restoration of the building revealed the presence of the original wattle chimney shaft with soot still clinging to the centre and a later brick chimney built inside it, probably in the sixteenth century. Another was found intact in the Bromsgrove house re-erected at Avoncroft Museum, Stoke Prior, Worcestershire (Plate 8).

With the improvement in social conditions it was not long before the simple recessed fireplace found its way from the manor to the home of the yeoman and the cottager, where it became its most important feature, the very heart of family life. It was like a self-contained kitchen, as much as 10ft wide in some yeomen's houses and 6–7ft wide in cottages and half as deep, occupying practically the whole of one wall. It often had seats built within it and a bread oven in one wall (Plate 2). It had a bar for suspending a spit or stock-pot, as well as all kinds of cooking and stoking utensils. There would often be a recess in the wall near the hearth where the salt could be kept dry; it was known as the salt box.

Necessity being the mother of invention, various expedients were used to solve problems created by the chimney. Bacon, previously cured anywhere in the room, was placed in a special smoke chamber leading off the flue; and a parallel to the modern under-floor draught system has been found in some seventeenth-century chimneys in the form of a small duct through the brickwork to provide sufficient draught to carry away smoke and help the fire to burn. Later innovations included a spit turned by means of a belt attached to a propeller up the flue, the propeller itself being turned by the rising hot air.

In general these homely fireplaces were so useful and became so much a part of the life of the farmhouse and cottage that they were scarcely affected by the change of design which came about in the great houses as the Renaissance movement was beginning.

Chimneys

The chimney developed from a simple flue in the wall into an imposing stack, a dominating feature which was as much a sign of social progress in those days as a colour television set is today. At first they were additions to rather than integral parts of many buildings, great two-storied stacks containing fireplaces for the parlour and the chamber, being added to external walls; later they became part of the general design of the house.

The sixteenth-century brickmaker produced some of the most beautiful and distinctive chimneys of any age. With consummate skill he moulded and shaped the clay before it was fired, using an axe for the fine scorings with which he decorated it and a float-stone for smoothing it. The tall twisted chimneys of the early Tudor manor house became a familiar part of its design. The owner's status was shown by the number of chimneys, for by this time not only the great hall but every room of importance was expected to have a fireplace.

The yeoman farmer was not slow to copy this idea, and soon his farmhouse displayed a massive stack in the form of a cluster of chimneys, often beautifully ornamented. Each chimney might be patterned differently and set diagonally or square, completed with mouldings, but the favourite was still the spiral. At Steventon in Berkshire there is one of these clusters in brick, all of different designs, with a huge chimney breast to the street, an obvious seventeenth-century addition to the medieval house. In Kent and Sussex a plain stack was the fashion.

On some of the lesser halls made into farmsteads these graceful and varied chimney stacks make an imposing finish to an old timber building; but on smaller houses such elaboration looks overpowering. This is clearly demonstrated on a row of small houses in Albury, Surrey, though the designs of the chimneys are so attractive that without them the little houses would lose any claim to distinction.

An outside stack on a yeoman's house could be of considerable width, perhaps 8–10ft and there were spaces on either side of it. The space at the front was used as an entrance lobby and the other one took the newel stairway.

This was the general arrangement until the early seventeenth

century when the introduction of balloon framing meant that the
floor had no part in carrying the upper storey, as it did in jettied
construction, and the joists could now be 'trimmed' to take an
integral chimney stack (see Fig 25). It was a major step forward, for
it meant that the stack could be put inside the house where it would
warm the building far more effectively. From this time onwards we
see some fine central chimney stacks, particularly in farmhouses
where the great open fire was used for a variety of purposes. If the
stack was placed between the hall and the parlour, there could now
be a fireplace on each side, one for each room; the yeoman could at
last enjoy the comfort and privacy of his fireside away from the sight
and smell of the cooking, for most farmers' wives did their cooking
in the hall—very few had a separate kitchen as yet.

Another great advantage of this arrangement was that the framed
staircase could now safely be placed beside the stack, which partly
supported it. But there are always exceptions. There are some early
examples in which the stack is at the end of the hall and not central,
such as that at Synyards (Plate 7). Here the huge open brick fireplace,
which had a bread oven at the side, was placed in the hall at the
opposite end to the screens passage, and it had another fireplace
backing on to it in the adjoining parlour. The same stack serves a
fine stone fireplace in the bedroom above. The openings each side of
the hall fireplace are taken up by the Tudor doorway to the parlour
at the front of the house, and the great oak dog-leg stairway on the
other side.

The new design spread from the south-eastern counties to the
Midlands and as far as the Welsh border by the eighteenth century.
Meanwhile the chimney stack had lost some of the ornate late-Tudor
carving and had become plainer. It was a massive structure, either
rectangular or cruciform, or simply circular, with the cap in the form
of a classical order with projecting courses of bricks. On Moat Farm,
Dormston, Worcestershire, there is a fine central chimney stack with
star-shaped tops (Plate 6). In East Anglia the builders showed a
preference for diagonal chimneys, sometimes varied by a peculiar
zigzag form. In areas where the Flemings settled there are some
unusual crow-stepped chimneys, a design which is rarely repeated in
other places.

The humble cottages did not aspire to such luxuries as moulded brickwork and decoration, except perhaps for plain projecting courses, but they always managed to look very charming and original. Many country cottages of the sixteenth and seventeenth centuries have big outside chimney stacks, some with a bake-oven built on to the base under a kind of lean-to roof. One is shown in Plate 21 and there is another to be seen on a delightful timber-framed and thatched cottage at Eardisland, Herefordshire.

Timber-frame building had declined by the time of the Anglo-classic, or Queen Anne and Georgian periods, so the new fireplace designs that were inspired for the first time by individual architects played little part in it. Apart from the constant addition to old buildings it remained for the Victorian small house owner to disfigure and debase the traditional open brick fireplace by closing it in and installing a hideous cast-iron grate in a tiny opening. Still later came the dreary beige-tiled fireplace of the early twentieth century, and unfortunately many old timber-frame cottages were fitted with them. Fortunately the nineteenth-century improvers seldom did anything more drastic than to fill in the original wide brick fireplace with rubble and many have been rediscovered and restored to their former state by the removal of these additions.

SEVEN

Roofing

In the beginning, when man first emerged from his cave, his first 'house' was, in effect, a roof, rising direct from the ground, a crude tent-shaped hut of the kind described in Chapter One. The hut which evolved from this wigwam type had a roof consisting of a strong ridge pole supported at each end by a pair of poles leant against each other and tied together at the top. If the ridge pole was longer than about 17ft an intermediate pole was used to prevent the structure from sagging. The rafter poles, which were necessary to carry the thatch, were arranged with their tops resting against the ridge pole and their feet embedded in the ground.

In course of time the pair of poles at each end of the hut became the crucks we have already mentioned, strong and handsome to look at, and carrying the whole weight of the roof. Some terminated at the apex, others were crossed with each other and pegged together to make a cleft in which to drop the ridge, or 'roof tree'. Each pair of crucks was strengthened by a horizontal tie-beam pegged into the members.

The roof rafters were made to rest on wall plates—stout beams—which were placed on the projecting ends of the tie-beam. Even when vertical walls were put up they still did not support the roof; the crucks and the tie-beams did that.

Strangely, the idea that heavy crucks were necessary to take the weight of the roof persisted in some parts of the country until well into the seventeenth century, when the 'post and truss' construction became generally used for timber-frame houses. This meant that the framing for the walls and the roof were at last completely separated.

Apart from cruck construction the early medieval roof did not have a ridge piece. The rafters were pitched one against the other in

'couples' and were tied about a third of the way down with horizontal timbers called collars to prevent spreading or sagging. This
relieved some of the strain on the apex, the remainder being taken by
the long beam placed under the collars which rested on to a crown-
post. Thus the weight was transferred down on to a tie-beam, which,
as well as taking the main weight of the roof to the wall frame, tied
it together, thus preventing the walls from bulging outwards.

A   Crown-post
B   Beam
C   Coupled rafters
D   Battens
E   Roof covering

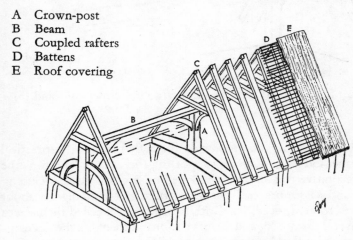

FIG 29   Medieval coupled roof

This arrangement prevented the roof from collapsing sideways,
but it was necessary to strengthen it further against the wind,
particularly in stormy areas. So further timbers, called wind braces,
were added where the joints were likely to be damaged by gale
buffeting. Wind braces are not only efficient but also decorative, and
assume pleasing, flowing shapes. They show up prominently on the
outside of a house. They are often seen on the type of yeoman's
house that has a recessed centre where the hall rose to the roof, as
curved braces supporting the roof over the recess and steadying the
structure against pressure from the end. These braces were obviously
necessary, for old records of wind damage show that a tempest in the
eleventh century blew down 500 houses in London alone.

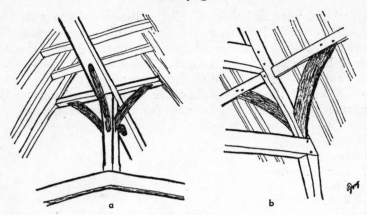

FIG 30　Braces on (a) fifteenth-century central crown-post and (b) sixteenth-century principal rafter

When the building was too wide for a tie-beam to be practical another method was found of supporting the rafters. This was the use of decorative trusses, also employed on cruck houses, including the arch and scissor braces. There is a certain grace and dignity about these early roofs. Indeed, the Gothic carpenters excelled themselves in design and execution, and we have to thank them for the development of the beautiful hammer-beam roof. Put simply, the rafters and collars were propped up by a kind of Gothic arch, that was supported on horizontal beams projecting from side walls. With their carved ornamental brackets these roofs are a splendid sight, particularly when the hammer beams are arranged in tiers. This kind of construction was, of course, only seen in large houses, like the manor houses and their banqueting halls, where they were a magnificent feature. Though it is not a house, Westminster Hall, London, shows the hammer-beam roof in all its glory. It was built in 1394-9 by a master carpenter, Hugh Harland, for Richard II, and has a span of 68ft.

Decorative trusses were, of course, expensive both in time and materials. It was found unnecessary to use them on every pair of rafters, and so they gradually came to be reserved for the principal rafters which were set at specific intervals along the roof, the spaces between being known as bays. The trusses were then connected to each other longitudinally by a ridge piece and purlins, and lighter common rafters were placed on these to carry the laths and roof covering.

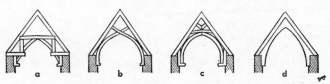

FIG 31   Ornamental trusses: (a) hammer beam, (b) scissor, (c) arch braced, (d) arch

The idea of using principals spread to the smaller houses, where it was used with a king-post and tie-beam truss in place of the more expensive trusses used in large buildings. As before, the trusses were linked by the ridge piece and purlins that ran the length of the building, the wind braces being inserted between the principal rafter and purlin, not on the crown-post as in the coupled roof. The massive principals were firmly secured to the post, wall plate, and tie-beam by an interlocking mortise joint (Fig 32) and the central truss, usually made of heavier timbers than the ends, was sometimes given added support by an arch brace between the posts and the tie-beam, as was the tie-beam of the coupled roof. Later the queen-post truss was used for the central truss, with some advantages when the hall ceased to be open to the roof and the attic room came into use.

Various combinations of all these beams, collars, and posts may be found, seemingly depending on the whim or technique of the builder, house owner, or local tradition. The design was often influenced by the available timbers, though the system was usually logical, as a study of the medieval roof will prove. There was little or no scientific knowledge, but construction was based on common sense and past experience.

Roofs were not always left open, of course. During the fifteenth century it became the fashion to have a roof boarded, or to give it a ceiling. Sometimes the tie-beams were left visible, and the rafters

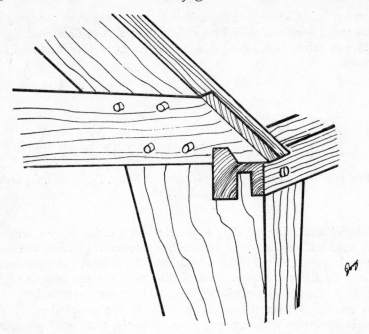

FIG 32   Joint tying tie-beam to principal rafter and wall plate

and braces were concealed by what was called a false roof. In wealthy homes it would be elaborately decorated, with various carvings called bosses and keys at the junction of the panels dividing the ceiling. By the sixteenth century the timbered roof, with all its variations of light and shade and its hint of mystery, had disappeared from the domestic scene.

Externally, the shape of a roof can give a clue to the design of a house and add character to the structure. In the Middle Ages buildings tended to be long and narrow, with the roof ending in

Ceiling and wall decoration. Plate 25 (*above left*) Medieval collared roof timbers, ceiled in Kent; Plate 26 (*above right*) moulded Tudor beams, Kent; Plate 27 (*below*) Ceiling embellished with moulded ribs and moulded and traceried beams, with early sixteenth-century wall panelling in the entrance hall of Tolleshunt D'Arcy Hall, Essex

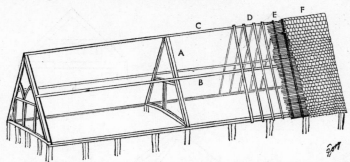

FIG 33   Trussed rafter roof construction. (A) Trussed principal rafters;
(B) Purlins; (C) Ridge piece; (D) Common rafters; (E) Battens; (F) Roof
covering

gables. Indeed, the problem of roof construction in those early days limited the size of most buildings to the span of one room in thickness, ie the length of the tie-beam. When future generations came to enlarge these buildings the easiest way was to build on an additional bay, with the roof extended over it. Many cottagers added a boarded lean-to at the side, framed on upright posts, with the roof continuing almost to the ground in a sweeping 'catslide'. Sometimes a series of sheds would be built on to the back of a house, to form a scullery, wash house etc, making a further diversion in the roof line. Add to this a few dormers, each with its gable, put in when an attic was needed or more head room wanted, and one gets the picturesque jumble of roof tops which can be seen in any village street. It adds to the charm and variety of the scene but it makes it practically impossible to date any of the buildings without studying the timbers underneath.

When square houses came to be built during the Renaissance period the roof ran all round the sides of the square, and where it met at the ridges it became the 'hips'. Smaller houses, with a ridge, might still have the gable ends 'hipped back'. In Kent it is typical of the

Additional cladding. Plate 28 (*above*) Tile hanging on weathered timbers at 'Wards-brook', Ticehurst, Sussex; Plate 29 (*below*) partially weatherboarded and brick-filled weavers' cottages, Goudhurst, Kent

G

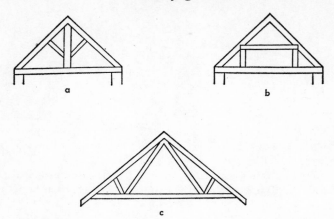

FIG 34   Trussed rafters: (a) king-post, (b) queen-post, (c) modern
truss

larger house to be hipped at both ends, but East Anglia has a
preponderance of steep gables, and, on occasion, the more un-
common mansard roof.

The buildings of gables often meant that the butt ends of the roof
timbers were exposed, so these were protected by 'barge' boards.
Those early craftsmen, who gloried in their skill, soon made these
boards into a decorative feature, sometimes piercing them to make
lace-like patterns, or leaving them plain with curved edges, a design

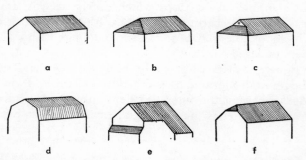

FIG 35   Roof shapes: (a) gabled, (b) hipped, (c) gambrel, (d) mansard,
(e) lean-to and catslide, (f) hipped gable

seen mostly in East Anglia. Sometimes these boards were enriched
with delicate tracery and beautiful carved designs of trailing foliage.
The oak, the rose, the hawthorn, and pomegranate were familiar
favourites. In Shrewsbury, where decoration tends to be lavish, the
trailing vine is used to great effect, with gable finials taking the form
of knights and ladies with pendants of a man's head (Plate 35). The
niche was another popular form of decoration, used for the ends of
wall posts under roofs. The figure within the niche was sometimes
of a religious character or sometimes a knightly one. There are very
few examples left intact, but one may be lucky enough to come
across one here and there.

Roof Coverings

Thatch, shingles, stone slates, geological slates, tiles, and pantiles—
all of these are in use on timber-frame houses, and, with few exceptions, all look right in their particular setting.

One cannot talk too strictly about the right materials for the right
locality these days when houses in one area are reaching out to those
in another. Nevertheless, one still looks for stone in the Cotswolds,
in Horsham and other parts of Sussex, and locally in the north; for
slate in Wales and the Lake District—away from the Limestone Belt;
for tiles in the south-east and Midland areas; and for thatch, the
traditional roofing of timber-frame building wherever it is to be
found.

A thatched cottage has come to be regarded the world over as one
of the endearing features of the English countryside, as much a part
of the scene as the village green and the church. The attachment is
not entirely sentimental, for thatch—or 'thack', as it was originally
called—has proved its worth over some thousands of years and is
still a first-rate roofing material. It is good to look at, durable,
completely weatherproof, the perfect insulator, and eminently practical. It is fast coming back into favour. For many years it was looked
down on as the poor man's roofing material, so much so in the
class-conscious eighteenth and nineteenth centuries that many people
tiled that part of the roof which was visible from the road and
thatched the rest. One such example is still to be seen on the outskirts
of Orpington, Kent. This prejudice vanished when Welsh slates
became plentiful and cheap early in the last century and thatching

became by comparison much more expensive. Slate, like thatch, replaced other materials in the front of some houses near Welshpool, but the back was left as stone.

The fear of fire in thatched roofs was no doubt justified in the days of roaring wood fires and soot-encrusted wattle chimneys. A long iron pole and hook was used to rake off burning thatch quickly, and one of these implements is still to be seen at Thaxted Guildhall. But the risk of fire has been greatly reduced with modern methods of control and fire-retardants.

Thatching is, of course, one of the oldest building crafts in Britain, in practice very little changed since the Middle Ages. It defies mechanisation. The tools needed are simple, often made by the thatcher himself, and vary from county to county as do the methods of work and the technical terms employed.

Briefly, the thatch is sewn to the roof battens with tarred cord in a special stitching needle, or fixed to the common rafters with hazel rods and hooks. The rods and hooks are then covered by the topmost layer, until the last coat of thatch is pinned to the roof ridge. The thatcher works from the eaves upwards, spreading his material and raking it, or combing it, to an even surface—upwards for reed and downwards for straw. It would be interesting to work out, for instance, why gable ends, dormers and roof ridges are treated differently in each county, and why their shapes differ.

Thatching Materials

Until the introduction of burnt clay, stone or slate, thatch in one form or another was the only roofing material available other than wood. Reeds, rushes, broom, heather, and even bracken were used before cultivated barley, wheat, and rye straw came into being.

At first the straw was rough and difficult to harvest, but early in the last century instruments were devised for combing wheat straw to produce the clean straight stems known as wheat reed. In more recent years the use of the combine harvester, and the trend for farmers to grow short straw varieties of wheat, has forced the thatcher to look for other materials. The best and most lasting of these is the marsh reed of Norfolk. It grows wild in vast quantities in the Norfolk marshland and the tidal estuaries of Suffolk, Essex,

Dorset, and other places where low-lying saltings are to be found. Today it is the most highly prized material and it is ironical to reflect that with all the modern technical advances in farming we should in the end return to the earliest of nature's thatching material.

Norfolk reed is tough and will not bend easily, so sedge is used for ridging purposes. It is very pliable and when it matures it turns to a beautiful golden brown. Both in tone and texture it sets off the beauty of the light golden Norfolk reed roof. A Norfolk reed thatch has to be 'dressed' (Plate 16) into position, which gives it a neat close-cropped look. Its cap of sedge, in a clean-cut pattern, secured with hazel cross-sparring, keeps it weatherproof.

Combed wheat reed, which is most widely used in the south-east of England, and sometimes called Devon reed, looks like Norfolk reed from a distance, with the same neat close-cropped finish, but closer inspection shows that the eaves and gables of wheat reed are cut to shape—a distinction between the two techniques. The method of thatching is the same with the two materials, both being laid 'reed wise' with the butts of the stalks showing. Nowadays wheat reed is combed by machine, which removes the grain and leaves from the wheat. The straw comes from the machine undamaged, with the butts laid in one direction. The straw reed and the water reed shed water in the same way, the drops of moisture dripping from stalk to stalk instead of running down the solid outer surface.

Another type of thatching, which may be seen in most of the corn-growing counties, is known as *long straw*. It has its own distinctive features, which are easy to recognise. It is applied to the roof in yealms (ie prepared layers of wetted straw, 14–18in wide and 4–6in thick) and is not dressed into position. It gives the impression of having been poured over the roof, following any slight irregularities without a break, with a pleasing, flowing effect. Eaves and gables in long straw are nearly always decorated with a pattern of ornamental hazel rods, as a means of fixing the thatch. This is not seen with the reed-laying techniques. The ridge may be decorated or flush, according to choice.

A roof has to have a properly constructed framework on to which thatch can be fastened and the rafters are much more widely spaced than for a tiled roof. A master thatcher may often be called upon to do a little carpentry to overcome problems of pitch, or he may be required to build a new gable. Rarely does he resort to the services of a carpenter.

The old English foundation to a thatched roof was wattle instead of laths, and we have been interested to discover this type of structure on many old roofs when they have been under repair or stripped for re-roofing. One such was found at Apple Tree Cottage, Quarley, Hampshire, where the original support was a very rough wattling, held down to the roof timbers by a triangular piece of wood through which a peg was driven (Plate 19). The wattle was black and brittle with age and smoke, yet still holding together firmly when it was removed.

There is another type of thatching, known as *wood chip*, which still exists on some very old houses in parts of Sussex, though the method is dying out. The thatch is made from lengths of wood, which used to be offcuts from hoops made of hazel or chestnut split down the centre (a stick 2–3in in diameter) and then shaved, trimmed and tapered at both ends for approximately 3ft. The wedges of wood are bundled up with other shavings and the tapered lengths are used with the large end of the taper on the outside of the roof, making the bundles wedge type, like Norfolk reed, with the same diameter on the inside of the roof. The tool used is very similar in principle to the legget used in reed-thatching, and the chip thatch is sewn down in the same way with tarred string. As with reed, the more the roof covering is beaten up the tighter the chips become. Since hoops are no longer made, the thatcher has to make his own wood chips on the rare occasions when he is called upon to do so.

The survival of such an individual craft as thatching in the face of modern competition owes much to the Rural Industries Bureau (now The Council of Small Industries in Rural Areas—CoSIRA) and the use of mechanical aids for the harvesting of materials.

The length of life of a thatched roof depends on a number of factors. If it is sheltered from prevailing winds or not under tall trees where drippings will encourage moss to grow, a Norfolk reed thatch can last 100 years. (We have been told of instances of a longer life than this, but had no means of checking.) Combed wheat reed may last for upwards of fifty years and long straw thirty-five years. CoSIRA says that its durability also depends on the quality of the crop and materials, weather conditions, and, most important of all, the skill of the thatcher. Supposing all these conditions to be favourable, a thatched roof will give complete satisfaction and a warm and cosy look that no other material ever quite achieves.

Shingles, or wooden tiles

We first hear of shingle roofing in Anglo-Saxon times, particularly for churches. The carpenters then were very adept in their use of timber. They split the parts of a tree unsuitable for beams into shingles, and cut them by hand in such a way that the grain of the wood served as tiny spouts for the water. They overlapped them in a neat pattern on the steeply pointed roofs, so that no snow could drift in between them and no rain could penetrate.

In medieval times shingles were still used widely, though they were never as popular as thatch. A sharp rise in the cost of timber between the fifteenth and sixteenth centuries made them uneconomic. Their durability was unquestionable; some fifteenth-century oak shingles can still be found in remarkably good condition, mellowed and weathered to a deep silvery grey (Plate 18).

For a time the use of shingles ceased, but now, with a newly awakened interest in timber building, Canadian cedar shingles are coming to the fore. On old cottages, where the roof was previously thatched and the rafters are not strong enough to take heavy tiles, shingles can be the ideal compromise (Plate 21). When new, they are usually sprayed with a wood preservative to prevent woodworm, and in time they weather to a silvery grey so that they harmonise with any setting. They have an average life of fifty years and cost very little more than tiles. Their main drawbacks seem to be the risk of fire and the slightly higher insurance premium demanded, and, in some places, restrictions imposed by local by-laws.

Stone Slates

They were one of the earliest forms of roofing, apart from thatch. The Romans frequently used stone to roof their houses, the earliest of which were timber-frame. Sometimes they used hexagonal slabs of stone, secured with hand-made iron nails of the kind which were not used again for several centuries.

Today stone is plentiful in parts of the north of England and in those regions covered by the great limestone belt, from Dorset to

East Yorkshire, including Herefordshire and Welsh Border Counties (Plate 17). Horsham (and elsewhere in Sussex) is also noted for its stone; indeed, Horsham stone is one of the finest roofing materials available, being practically indestructible.

The heavier varieties of stone slab from the north need a strong timber frame to support them, with a fairly low pitch to the roof. They are hung on to the laths by means of pegs driven into holes near the top edge of the tile. They are usually laid in diminishing courses, growing gradually smaller from eaves to ridge, that is, the heaviest stones are laid just above the eaves, so that the walls take the weight of them, the next in weight are laid above them, overlapping the ones beneath, and so on, until the ridge is reached. The ridge is normally formed out of solid sawn or split stone.

In medieval days the stones were bedded on moss, and the lowest layers were pointed on the underside to keep the roof watertight. The tile pins were made of oak, a practice which present-day craftsmen condemn as unsatisfactory, possibly explaining the frequent repairs to roofs mentioned in old accounts. Earthen tiles were hung in the same way; and when an old building is being demolished one often comes across tiles or stone slates with the wooden pegs still in them.

The old-time slaters in the Cotswolds used a language of their own to describe the kind of slate they were using, its size, and weight. Some of these names were as quaint and imaginative as those the weavers inscribed on their bobbins; for instance, these were Bachelors, Movedays, Rogue-why-winkest-Thou, Jenny-why-Gettest-Thou, Short Backs, Long Backs, Shorts save one, and many others.

When old stone slates are fixed on hand-riven timber they have a gentle, wavy irregularity, and often a dappling of green and gold lichen adds to their venerable appearance. With all this, they are highly practical on any house in an exposed place. Being non-conductors of heat, they keep a house cool in summer and warm in winter. But, sadly, they are no longer economic and have largely given way to the manufactured concrete tile.

Slates Proper are seen in many forms on timber-frame buildings, from the small rough slates used in Wales and Westmorland before the Industrial Revolution to the large thin machine-split slates which superseded them when large-scale mechanical production and easier transport became available. The original hand-made slates, with their slight irregularity, look infinitely better than machine-split slates on a traditional timber-frame building, the old style of slate seeming to complement the old style of building.

True slate comes from the Cambrian and Silurian rock formations. To fulfil its purpose it must be hard and fissile, in colour varying from grey and green to blue or black. The quality and texture of roofing slates differ a good deal, depending on the locality from which they come. Those from Bangor in North Wales are a dull blue-purple colour; Irish slates are somewhat tougher and heavier; and English slates from Westmorland, Lancashire and Cornwall are thick, with a rough surface and jagged edges, and a beautiful grey-green colour.

The trade names for slates were ladies, viscountesses, countesses, duchesses, princesses, and queens, according to their size, and also 'doubles'. They are used in a similar way to stone slates, on a roof of fairly low pitch, and laid in courses with the longest next the eaves and the shortest at the ridge. Being less absorbent than tiles, slates are better for buildings in exposed places, but being conductors of heat they do not add to the comfort of a home.

Tiles

They almost displaced thatch on timber-frame houses at one time, particularly in towns, where the risk of fire was great. As early as 1212 Londoners were forbidden to use 'Straw, Reeds, Rushes or Strubble' on roofs because of fire risks. By the beginning of the thirteenth century the making of clay tiles was well established, but they were not easy to come by as time went on because of the amount of fuel needed for the manufacture of the burnt clay, and did not become a common form of roofing until the early seventeenth century. Some medieval records tell us of transgressors being fined not in money but in tiles, which is a fair indication of their value at that time.

Celia Fiennes records in her *Journeys of Celia Fiennes* (1685–98): 'In Bury St. Edmunds the old houses of timber and mostly in the old forme of the country which are long peaked roofs of tileing.' There are still plenty of old tiled roofs in East Anglia, particularly on farmhouses. As they grow older they tend to develop a patina of lichen and moss, and in Kent, parts of Surrey, and Sussex they often form part of a picturesque medley of thatched and stone roofs.

A tiled roof is steeply pitched in order to keep the rain out. In the past, when thatching was looked down on, many people converted their thatched roofs to tiling, but nowadays this can be an expensive business. The pitch has to be changed and new timbers substituted for the original rough supports. In many ways it is better to keep to the original material when a new roof is needed on an old timber-frame house.

Modern concrete tiles never seem to mellow or weather with age as did their clay prototypes, though they are now made in a variety of soft colourings which look quite pleasing. They are used frequently on the new style of timber-frame house, where they blend in well enough with the up-to-date forms of cladding.

Pantiles, though of comparatively recent introduction in England, were the Roman form of tile. Among the building materials listed in the Roman Villa at Bignor, Sussex (excavated in 1811), are 'Innumerable tiles, varying in size from 6 inch squares to enormous burnt clay slabs for floors, hypocausts and roofing'. But the present pantile probably bears little resemblance to its Roman prototype. It has a flowing ogee shape, which can look very neat and distinctive on a timber-frame house of any period. It varies a good deal in shape and colour. Some very bright colours are used today, unfortunately not always in harmony with Nature's own colours in the countryside. In East Anglia a dull or slightly glazed black is often seen, striking a sympathetically sombre note in a part of the country where the weather can be harsh.

Finally, there is the asbestos tile, a post-war product that does not mellow with age and so tends to clash with its surroundings. It is, of course, fireproof, but because of its tendency to explode in fierce heat it is not always the best roofing to have in case of fire.

We said before that it is the roof which helps to give character to a timber-frame house. If that is so, the supreme example of vacillation could be seen in 1969 in a tiny Kentish village, where a small cottage had begun by wearing a cap of thatch, had changed to earthen tiles round the small dormers, had acquired a large patch of slates at one end, and then a sheet of corrugated iron at the other. In its semi-wild surroundings the effect was wholly delightful.

EIGHT

Cladding and Decoration

One of the most endearing aspects of traditional timber-frame building is the way in which it lends itself to an infinite variety of cladding materials and decoration, both inside and out. Each county has its own distinctive style, dictated to a certain extent by the availability of local materials, but even more by the personal methods and preferences of the builder, whose work thus seems to be a natural corollary to the surrounding landscape.

Exterior Cladding
The Anglo-Saxon way of making a wall was to erect rows of rough sawn or split planks, at first just planted into the ground and later mortised top and bottom into horizontal beams, a method known as bratticing, which also served for exterior walling of internal partitions. Towards the end of the twelfth century, when joinery techniques improved, it became possible to make proper frames, and studs took the place of planks, the spaces between them filled with wattle and daub. Wattling consisted of upright stakes interlaced with hazel rods, brushwood, reeds, or any similar pliant material, to form a close hurdling. Such materials, collected from the woods nearby, have been recovered hundreds of years later complete with bark and lichen attached. The uprights were usually oak stakes fitted into mortises at the top and grooves in the lower horizontal member, but hazel wands or sticks pliable enough to be sprung into holes in the timbers have been used. In some Shropshire houses birch, stripped of its bark, or oak were used. These uprights were too stiff to be sprung into place in the holes used top and bottom and the rods seem to have been pushed up into extra deep holes and then pulled down into position. In these cases the wattles were split oak or beech laths

interlaced between the uprights, but more generally the wattles were hazel or birch, whatever the stakes may have been (Plate 11).

The composition of the daub varied. Clay was used, and some of the earliest forms were simply made of mud and cow dung, which contained a certain amount of straw; but tow or hair from virtually any animal was used equally well as a binding agent. The daub was thrown on each side of the wattling and pressed well into all the crevices to form a thick stout screen. It was done in layers, each layer being left to dry before the next one was applied. When the clay mixture dried it was apt to shrink and crack, so a thin coat of lime plaster mixed with cow hair was applied to seal the cracks and give a better finish. At a later date split laths, usually of oak, were used instead of wattles, with a coat of plaster to strengthen them, followed by a liberal daubing of whitewash. The builder of the Middle Ages was very partial to whitewash, which was often applied to the mud and clay mixture.

At first these panels were thinly covered, giving the appearance of being recessed into the timbers sometimes to the depth of an inch, but in later medieval buildings they are often seen to be flush with the studs, giving a more substantial and smooth surface, possibly due to the practice of merely adding another layer when repairs were necessary.

This traditional method of cladding persisted for centuries and was so satisfactory that the rural builders stuck to it long after more sophisticated ways had been introduced. Many an old timber-frame house today has its original wattle and daub walls intact, preserved under successive coats of plaster and acting as a perfect insulator. A particularly fine set of panels was found during restoration at Bromesberrow (Plate 11) where it is possible to see that the wattling could be applied to fill a space of any shape.

Plastering

Closely connected with daubing, it has been used as an external sheath since early Jacobean times. It has been said that it was a device to conceal the scanty timbers which were used at this time of scarcity, but the fact that so many earlier houses, some of the fifteenth and sixteenth centuries, hide their timber frames beneath a plaster cladding, does not support this theory.

Plaster was used extensively in East Anglia and this suggests that its main purpose was weatherproofing not disguise. There are, however, some houses of a later date, probably late seventeenth century, which were intended to be plastered from the first and are only roughly timbered, but this can only be discovered as a rule when the timbers are uncovered for repair work. This old plaster was composed of lime and sand and bound with finely teased cow or horse hair, cleaned of all dirt. It all had to be passed by the master builder and it was so well mixed and beaten that it became stronger as the years passed. It was applied to a layer of split laths, usually oak, fixed with nails to the outside face of the timbers, not between them as with wattle and daub. The surface was finished with a coat of whitewash or colourwash in light pinks, greens, or blues, which look quite charming beneath a thatched roof. Some of the most beautiful villages and hamlets in southern Suffolk consist almost entirely of these timbered and colourwashed cottages, but, of course, the timbering is masked by the sheath of lath and plaster. There is a lovely triangular group with thatched roofs near the church at Cavendish, Suffolk; and another couple at Battisford, with tiny dormers set in a steeply pitched roof covering the white plastered walls.

Smaller cottages are generally plain but a few share the distinction of larger houses and farmhouses in displaying some fine ornamental plasterwork, known as pargeting. The original intention of this bas-relief exterior was to break the fall of the rain and to save the plaster from disintegrating as it ran down the walls—a delightful way of achieving such a utilitarian purpose. In Hereford and Worcester tiled projections on walls produce the same effect (Plate 6). In the main, the craftsmen responsible for much of this pargeting came from the Low Countries, and this accounts for its prevalence in East Anglia, where they settled.

The pargeting on cottages is mainly in the traditional pricked or combed patterns, such as scalloped circles, crows' feet or cables; but occasionally the plain plaster elevation of a row of cottages is broken by a decorative strip of pargeting in leaf motif, as at Sibton, Suffolk, or at Bishop Bonner's cottage at East Dereham, Norfolk, where there is a very fine decorative frieze in a floral design. More ambitious designs were used on larger houses, where the craftsman had room to indulge his artistic fancies. One which sets every tourist's camera clicking is the white plastered house opposite the church at Clare, Suffolk, in spite of the distinctly unpicturesque iron railings round the churchyard. The front elevation is lavishly pargeted in a sculptured floral design which forms a setting for two graceful oriel windows, one set beneath the jettied gable and the other in the gable itself. A second gable at the end is more simply ornamented with a shield set in a circle above a simple design of leaves and the date 1473. This is obviously the date of the original part of the building and not that of the pargeting, which was done when the plaster sheath was applied, much later.

Ipswich shows some interesting examples of moulded plasterwork, which tends to be rather more lavish here than in other parts of the county. The sixteenth-century Ancient House, now the Deben Bookshop but more familiarly known as Sparrowe's House, after an early owner, has some unrivalled pargeting ornamenting the entire façade, and this, with the decorative timbering at ground level, makes it a showpiece of the county. The house has five oriel windows, four facing the Butter Market and one in St Stephens Lane on the west front. Beneath the windows and on the panels between them are some plaster emblems representing Europe, Asia, Africa, and America, and on the west side are a figure of Atlas supporting the world on his shoulders and a pastoral scene probably bearing some relation to the wool trade of which Ipswich was once the centre. Carved pendant strings of fruit and foliage decorate the entire width of the ground floor over the doors and windows, but the focal point above the main doorway is the Royal Coat of Arms of King Charles II, whom the Sparrowe family aided during his flight from his enemies (Plate 36). There is also some lavish pargeting on the walls of the courtyard at the back of the building, all of which is kept in excellent condition.

This very decorative form of plasterwork is achieved with the simplest of tools, mainly a fork-like comb for the combed patterns, a trowel, and a piece of rag. The art is not nearly as dead as some people would have us believe; there are still some rural craftsmen in East Anglia who design and fashion beautiful ornamental plasterwork with no more than the skill of their hands and a few simple tools.

Another form of plaster cladding is rough-cast or stucco, whereby lime mortar or a coarse form of plaster is used with sand or small pebbles thrown on to it to make a rough surface. It became popular during the Regency and many an old timber-frame house in need of weatherproofing was thus treated.

Brick

It has been used as an infilling with timber-framing since it became generally available in the fifteenth century. The practice was known as 'brick nogging' and was at first used in East Anglia and the Home Counties (round London), bricks having been brought into the country as ballast in ships. At first it was a luxury, but after 1660 brick nogging replaced wattle and daub as a form of cladding. The bricklayer, a craftsman in his own right, displayed much ingenuity in the arrangement of the bricks. The earlier bricks, as already noted in a previous chapter, were small and rosy red in colour and were often laid in herring-bone pattern or diagonally. In the close-timbered houses of Essex and Suffolk it is common to see a filling of one layer of bricks set at angles, zigzag fashion, between the studs, and, where the space is wider, another layer set in herring-bone pattern, with the mortar bonding forming a perfect design of clean-cut joints. In the house at Lavenham (Plate 12) the brick nogging is between close timbers. The nail marks visible on the studs indicate that at some time the building may have been clad with lath and plaster. It is easy to detect where the brick nogging has been renewed at different times by the different colours and varieties of the bricks and the way in which they have been set. In some cases a brick wall has been built to prop up an overhanging storey, and the work can often be dated by the size of the bricks.

Sometimes when a house was enlarged an entire elevation of brick would be superimposed on an old timber-frame structure to make it match the new part—as at Steyning in Sussex, where Chantry Green House, built in 1525, was enlarged in 1705 and a Queen Anne façade added to the original Tudor skin. In some parts of Sussex a rough flint infilling is seen, often in conjunction with wattle and daub or brick nogging, and it was obviously used only for repair, not complete restoration. All three methods are seen on the Old Shop, Bignor, Sussex (Fig 23), and in some areas stone was also used. In

Cheshire any type of infilling is described as 'nogging panes' and it is not always easy for the stranger to understand which kind is meant.

Tile-hanging

A very old architectural device to ensure a waterproof surface is hanging tiles on walls. In Anglo-Saxon days, according to some historians, it was a common practice to hang both roof and walls with wooden shingles, which were just as effective in keeping the rain out as were the later burnt clay tiles.

As time went on the wattle and daub filling of old timber-frame houses frequently shrank or cracked, or probably the house itself 'settled' on its foundations, causing some cracks in the plaster and threatening the timbers with rot. It then became imperative to find a way in which to preserve the structure from further damage and in certain localities tile-hanging was the chosen method, though it did not become general until tiles became cheaper and more available. It was well on in the seventeenth century before the cottager used them in this way, but by the eighteenth many timber-frame houses had disappeared under a layer of tiles. The tax on bricks, imposed by George III in 1784, caused a great increase in the use of tiles on exposed surfaces of walls; they were arranged to look like brickwork, and in this way the builders avoided the tax.

Wall tiles were slightly thinner than those used for roofs. They were hung on oak laths with wooden pins—usually oak, willow, or hazel—in overlapping rows, with occasional rows embedded in mortar. This produced a completely waterproof wall and an attractive one, particularly when the tiles mellowed to a deep red and took on a patina of greeny-grey lichen.

They were usually rectangular, but there is a surprising variety of patterns, some having half round ends, some with a flange at each side or with some other slight difference that marks them out for attention, giving a fish-scaled effect. Fish-scale tiles are seen a good deal on houses in Surrey and quite often the use of the different patterns is seen on the one house. Some people condemn this

---

Plate 30 (*above left*) Early fifteenth-century house frame at West Dean, Sussex; Plate 31 (*above right*) part of sixteenth-seventeenth-century frame at Bromesberrow, Herefordshire; Plate 32 (*below*) Erection of modern timber-frame house (*Frameform*) at Bedford

practice as being fussy, but the texture and colour of these old tiles is too subdued for them ever to become obtrusive.

Tile-hanging appears to be confined to the upper walls and gables while the ground floor is left in its former state. But in fact the use of tiles was purely functional and they were put where they were needed. Occasionally one sees a whole wing tile-hung, as at Shoyswell Old Manor, Sussex, where the east wing is in its original close-timbering with wattle and daub panels and the south wing and face is hung with tiles; or as at Ticehurst (Plate 28) where the weather sides are covered (these are usually east, south and west). Although north winds bring bad weather they do not apparently wreak as much havoc on old timbers as the sun.

The practice of tile-hanging is commonly found in Kent, Surrey, and Sussex, and in areas in Berkshire and Hampshire, but in very few other counties; certainly not in East Anglia, which seldom deviates from its characteristic plastering. Most houses having been clad before the inception of tile-hanging, it followed that when the brick tax was repealed in 1850 the use of wall tiles ceased and normal brickwork cladding again came into use.

Weatherboarding

Also called clapboarding, it was another method of weatherproofing exterior walls (see Chapter Five). It is a common cladding in Wales over houses originally square framed with wattle and daub infilling, but it is, of course, a very widespread device. Very occasionally elm boarding was used on cottages, with the wavy edges of the planks following the line of the growth of the tree. It looks attractively rustic, especially when the wood weathers to a russet or a silvery grey. In East Sussex and the Weald of Kent it is not unusual to see a combination of hanging tiles and tarred weatherboarding, the latter being a protective measure resorted to by boatmen who treated their houses as boats. Occasionally one sees a house that has resorted to all three methods, ie plastering, tile-hanging, and weatherboarding, giving an impression of indecision or excessive caution. A framed

Plate 33 (*above*) Double gable decoration over window at East Hagbourne, Berkshire; Plate 34 (*below*) decorated window, Lavenham, Suffolk

H

and weatherboarded lean-to, built on to the side of a cottage with wattle and daub walls, is another common sight and generally indicates that it was put up at a much later date than the house itself.

In north-east Hertfordshire the timbers were entirely concealed externally, either wholly by plaster or two-thirds by plaster with weatherboarding up to the ground-floor window sills (Plate 10). Sometimes the walls were entirely weatherboarded but the timber-framing was the same. In East Hertfordshire the panels between the timbers were usually wattle and daub with plaster rendering over all, but in the West Hertfordshire tradition the panels were more often filled with brick and the timbers left visible. Even when subsequently whitewashed and lightly plastered the method of construction is unmistakable.

Timber Decoration

Timber, being a natural material, is decorative enough in grain and texture, particularly when hand-worked. The wood carver came to the fore in a remarkable way during the fifteenth century, at a time when church building was on the wane and men began to think more of secular building. It was then that some of the beautiful Gothic detail wrought by the mason in the church began to be copied by the carver in wood, and houses were given a new dignity and rare beauty.

As with other features surrounding timber-frame building there were many regional characteristics applied to decoration in timber. There is, for instance, a marked difference in design and decoration in the north-western counties from the rest of England, particularly in the Tudor reigns, when they showed a great liking for heavy patterning. Panels filled in with a curved strut in each corner to make a simple lozenge design were general but in earlier work straight uprights and crossbars were used to make a diagonal design. It is not unattractive in small houses but becomes rather tiring to the eyes in a great house like Pitchford Hall, Shropshire. Chequerwork timbering is also a local peculiarity of Cheshire and parts of Lancashire in which each panel is made up of nine small squares or diamonds, five of plaster and four of oak. It is also common to see gables filled with angle struts springing from a centre post. In the south-east design was generally plainer but there were often some beautiful features singled out for special attention.

The first decoration was the simple chamfer on posts, doors and interior beams. The fifteenth-century carpenter also had a liking for moulding in straight, flowing lines to relieve the surface of his heavy timbers. Externally he used it on fascia boards to cover up the joist ends of an overhanging storey but at a later date he rounded off the ends of the timbers and left them exposed. He also used it on beams and corner posts to great effect.

Corner posts and brackets were often singled out for decoration, being favourite places for the house owner to display emblems of his position or his calling, so the adornment varies from a simple moulding on the end of a bracket to the elaborate and detailed series of carvings seen on many important buildings. A bracket on the Star Inn, Alfriston, Sussex, is beautifully carved and niched; it contains the mitred figure of St Giles, with the hind at his feet (Fig 36). On a corner post in Lavenham, Suffolk, where the teazel head curves outward to form a supporting bracket for the end of a dragon beam, there is a simple moulding topped by brattishing (a small type of battlementing—see Plate 24). The East Anglian tradition for symbolic ornamentation reaches its height in the Ipswich area, where a study of corner posts is an education in itself: on one a smith is depicted at work, close to his canopied fire; and on another the fable of the fox and geese is enacted.

They sometimes give us an inkling of the status of the original house owner. The fifteenth-century Abbot's House at Shrewsbury, for instance, has a fine square corner post with fillets on either side and a moulded capping over which the centre part, embellished with tracery, curves outwards. The fillets above the capping become brackets to support the overhanging storey above. The same theme is repeated in the next storey. There is a dignity and restraint about this design that is wholly in keeping with an ecclesiastical dwelling.

Brackets supporting an overhang were normally left plain or with very little adornment, but there are exceptions, and during the Renaissance some of the larger houses displayed carved mermaids, dolphins, or dragons within a circle of strapwork. Some of this more elaborate work is to be seen in Chester, but there has been so much

FIG 36   Carved bracket, Alfriston, Sussex

restoration that one must be careful to differentiate between the genuine and the false.

Beams were carved and decorated in a number of ways, one of which was tracery. This form of art became architectural in the fifteenth century and developed on geometrical lines, remaining so for about 150 years. Bresummer beams supporting the front of a building were often faced with a pattern of vertical and horizontal lines, sometimes elaborated with the curving ogee or cusped with roses. In Elizabethan times a diamond pattern was commonly used. Tracery was also used for panels and for barge boards, which have been mentioned in Chapter Seven, but it was seen at its best on windows when horn, or, later, glass was placed in the openings.

FIG 37   Window, The Porch House, Potterne, Wiltshire

Carvings are more commonly seen than tracery; some of the earliest were of a plaited design, starting from spirals like basket-work, and from this developed more natural floral designs and the lovely trailing vine which is repeated on beam, barge board, door head, or wherever there is carving to be seen. Sometimes religious texts or loyal sentiments were emblazoned on beams. On the front of God's Providence House, Chester, is carved the words 'God's

Providence is Mine Inheritance'. The beams are original but were restored in 1826. In another part of Chester there is a carving on a beam which says 'To My God, my King and my Country'.

Quatrefoiling was one of the commonest forms of ornamentation for the exposed faces of beams and barge boards, or sometimes for a filling. The medieval wood carvers may have taken their inspiration from the Roman form of quatrefoil with interlaced links, which is seen in various forms in their mosaic pavements (Fig 38), or from the popular guilloche, which is seen in modified forms in medieval art. The quatrefoil is an old design and one which is seen to somewhat startling effect on Little Moreton Hall, Cheshire, and in the heavily decorated black and white buildings in Shrewsbury. Owen's Mansion, which according to its carved stone was erected by Richard Owen, the Elder, Gentleman (a wealthy cloth merchant) in AD 1592, shows an abundance of sunken quatrefoils, with cusped concave braces and cable moulding (Plate 35).

The sunken quatrefoil is in fact only seen in houses in and near Shrewsbury built about 1570–95, which suggests it may have been the preference of one craftsman who worked in that area. Cable mouldings are often used with the quatrefoils or alone and were possibly the work of the same wood carver, though cable ornament is also seen in towns other than Shrewsbury.

FIG 38   Quatrefoil in Roman pavement, Bignor, Sussex

The top edge of a beam was sometimes decorated with brattishing, like mock battlements in miniature, and wall plates and camber beams were particularly suited to this kind of treatment, seen to advantage on manor houses or larger town houses. Normally, the yeoman had simpler tastes and did not decorate the exterior of his house to the same extent.

As *windows* developed and became more important, the builders sought to make them an attractive part of the design, and no window is more attractive than the graceful projecting oriel, which is such a charming feature of the sixteenth-century jettied house (Plate 34). The wood carver was able to work both on the brackets supporting the projection on the solid bases, which are a feature of the eastern counties, and on mullions. All manner of designs are carved on these bases, from simple floral patterns to heraldic devices with symbolic figure work, angels, bosses, and shields.

One superb carving is the inn sign on the 'White Swan' at Clare, Suffolk, which originally supported an oriel window. It dates from the early fifteenth century, and is done on a solid piece of wood measuring 9ft 8in by 2ft 4in. It portrays a chained swan between two conventional trees to which are attached small shields that appear to bear the arms of both French and English nobility. There is a similar fine carving on an oriel on the fifteenth-century Monk's House at Newport, Essex, depicting a Madonna-like figure rising from the clouds with a sceptre in hand and two angels playing heavenly instruments to make music for the Child. There are many other carvings whose symbolism is now incomprehensible, but the skill shown by their carvers and the obvious joy they had in their craft is sufficient for our enjoyment. In some parts the double gable achieves a very decorative effect, as seen at Drayton, Berkshire, where the oriel window rests on two simple brackets (Plate 33).

Doorways and porches were often profusely carved, with cables, mouldings or inscriptions. Carved figures at the side of a doorway often mean that the house originally belonged to a religious order. A fifteenth-century entrance might have a heavy oak nail-studded door, with moulded jambs and a carved lintel; or it might have the typical Tudor arch with oak jambs enriched by moulding (either hollow, ogee or round) and the door made of wide oak boards with concealed joins. Both these types are frequently seen in old manor houses of the late medieval period. The spandrels of the Tudor heads lent themselves to decoration and were seldom left unadorned. A doorway in Lavenham combines all the features we have described, and includes a wicket gate with an ogee head (Plate 12).

One type of sixteenth-century doorhead had a flattened four-centred arch within a rectangular frame. An individual type which was noted during restoration of a house at Braughing, Hertfordshire, was separate from the lintel and inserted like a valance in the doorhead, its narrow chamfer unconnected with the broad chamfer of the frame. This shape was peculiar to the house, a similar one being found carved with a lozenge motif in each spandrel; another, uncovered in a partition wall, had sunken spandrels carved with a leaf trail in the Gothic tradition but of debased design.

The Tudor style of building did not die with the age and one frequently sees a door of Tudor style, having a moulded label, in houses after 1660.

Heraldic bearings were an important part of medieval decoration, which later developed into a symbolic and complex art. Many of these coats of arms were brightly coloured and displayed prominently on the outside of buildings. At Shoyswell Old Manor, for instance, on a small ornamental pendant hanging from a barge board over a gable are the horse shoes of the Shoyswells upon the bend in their shield. It is possible that other heraldic bearings have been lost since the estate passed out of the hands of the family.

Interior Lining

Where wattle and daub was used for an infilling, the interior walls of a house looked much like the exterior, with the timbers showing between the panels, sometimes with a coat of whitewash or colour-wash for a finish. Where brick nogging was employed the interior walls were often plastered, with the timbers either left exposed or covered, according to the wish of the owner.

In the Middle Ages only external walls carrying the weight of the roof were built of load-bearing materials. When it came to sub-dividing the internal space into rooms, they used timber partitions made up of vertical boards fitted into horizontal beams top and bottom. These partitions could be placed edge to edge, tongued and grooved, with one side plain and the other side chamfered, or they could be feather edged. The boards could also be used horizontally, pegged to uprights that were fastened to the ground sill and top rail. Another method was bratticing, which in modern parlance is 'staggered' boarding, with fairly narrow planks placed at intervals and the gap between them filled with another board. This is like the stockade or breastwork of Anglo-Saxon days and is not often seen as an internal partition wall now; but there is a fine example in the Great Hall of Pattyndenne Manor, where a door of vertical planks looks as if it is a continuation of the panelling.

This bratticing was made of wainscot oak and by the sixteenth century it had developed into the kind of panelling that is familiar to us today. At first it was simply meant to conceal damp penetration and to insulate the house against cold, and everyone who could afford it panelled their rooms in wainscot oak; but it was not long before the wood carvers turned it into a decorative feature with characteristic touches which distinguish one era from another. For example, early Tudor panelling is mainly carved in a vertical mould-ing known as linen-fold from its appearance, and it was used on walls and doors alike; a practical point of this pattern was that the top sloped to prevent it harbouring too much dust. The Elizabethan style, however, is recognisable by its rows of squared-up panels some 10–14in wide and 11–15in high. It was well proportioned, with the wood carefully chosen for its grain, a simple style that remained almost standard for about a century and is still repeated to this day. In some wealthy houses the panels could be elaborated by the addition of mouldings within the frame to form an internal panel, diamond or lozenge shaped; others would insert some carving with conventional foliage or symbolic figures, the family's coat of arms being displayed prominently within the design.

The entrance hall or the middle room of the south wing of Tolleshunt D'Arcy Hall, Essex, is lined with early sixteenth-century panelling put in by Antony D'Arcy, Sheriff of Essex in 1512 (Plate 27). Most of it is linen-fold but at the top and near the middle of the walls the panels are carved with conventional foliage and various heads and figures described as a mermaid, an eagle, and a child (though the present owner inclines to the classical description of pygmies and cranes). Some panels have the initials A.D. for Antony D'Arcy and the lower ones bear the D'Arcy coat of arms. The whole is finished with an embattled cornice and two fine wall posts in the form of carved Ionic pilasters.

The Elizabethans had a passion for heraldry and would emblazon their walls with crests and shields of arms on bosses, cherubs, and the like. An embattled cornice frequently surmounted the rectangular panelling in more important rooms, providing a suitable finish to an imposing interior. In Jacobean times the trend was towards simplicity in the middling kind of house, and small framed panels covered the whole face of the wall. They were arranged in oblongs, to form a regular design, narrow and horizontal to about 3ft from the floor, above which they were vertical, broad and tall. Occasionally other woods besides oak were used, notably pine and chestnut, and often it was painted white.

Roof trusses often came in for their share of adornment and some were very ornate. In the Old Vicarage, Glasbury, Radnorshire, there is some varied cusping on the trusses and the arch braces are each finished with a carving at the bottom. On one is a female head with a square type of head-dress, while the other side has a male face complete with walrus moustache. On another brace is carved a mitred bishop holding a prayer-book—a fine piece of Welsh craftsmanship.

An early Tudor doorway had stop moulded jambs and beautifully carved spandrels of cusping or some other simple pattern which might well include a coat of arms. The door head was decorated with twisted mouldings or inscriptions with, perhaps, an embattled cornice to give it an imposing finish (Fig 39). Many an entrance to a Great Hall is ennobled in this way, with elaborately carved spere screens. Designs tended to grow more elaborate and flamboyant in the Elizabethan age, expressing the restless romantic spirit of the time, but the succeeding Jacobeans, from 1603 to 1625, were rather more crude in their interpretation though their basic style of decoration was similar. Many of their ideas came from Flemish sources and their detailing was often unfinished, but against this there was a strong move towards the Classical styles—Doric, Ionic, and Corinthian. Wall posts and crown- and king-posts carved to imitate stone pillars looked very dignified and beautiful in timber, and fortunately much of this work survives in timber-frame houses today.

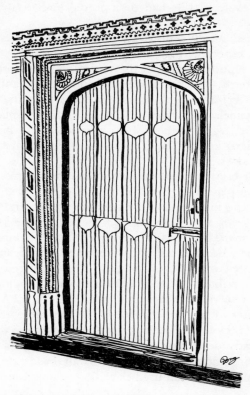

FIG 39   Decorated door, Tolleshunt D'Arcy Hall, Essex

Ceilings. In early days ceilings relied on their great oak beams for adornment, and the timbers which supported a medieval 'solar' were carved to form an ornamental ceiling to the parlour beneath. Sometimes the timbers were heavily moulded (as at Pattyndenne Manor, Plate 26) to reduce their oppressiveness, but as the beams became less massive the main ones were simply chamfered and the joists were left plain (Plate 25). In order that the ends of the beams should rest squarely on the wall plates or posts, the moulding or chamfering had to stop short of either end, and here the wood carvers designed an ornamental 'stop mould' as a final flourish. By the seventeenth century, however, all this had disappeared and the ceiling beams were left plain.

During the sixteenth century the carved wooden ceiling became very popular, especially for parlours, where the heavy timbers and battens that supported the medieval 'solar' were used to make attractive patterns. The beams were often moulded and elaborately carved (Plate 27) and at the intersections where the ceiling was divided into panels the wood carvers designed an ornamental stop moulding. The largest of these stops were known as bosses or keys and the smallest, knots. The Tudor rose was one of the favourite designs for a boss.

In yeomen's houses or small manors the beams sometimes framed panels of plain plaster—a moulded plaster ceiling was quite exceptional before the middle of the sixteenth century and the massive elaboration of this art affected timber-frame building very little.

One result of the Renaissance movement was the improvement of interior finishes. Beamed ceilings were covered with split laths and hard lime plaster, only the main beams being allowed to show. In better houses ceilings were embellished with moulded ribs and moulded and traceried beams in geometrical designs. A particularly beautiful ceiling of this kind is to be seen in the entrance hall of Tolleshunt D'Arcy Hall (Plate 27), complementing the wall panelling we have already described; it has moulded ribs in a geometrical design, and some moulded and traceried wall posts, one with cusped panelling, which have been used as ceiling beams to fine effect.

Interior Decoration

From Norman times there has been some attempt to beautify the house by what we now call 'interior decoration'. The first wall coverings in feudal manor houses were tapestry or arras, with pictures of battles and great events illustrated in fine needlework; their main purpose was to keep out the draughts, but they also had great artistic merit and, now, historic value. A more modest version of the costly tapestry hanging was the painted cloth, a type of wall decoration common in Tudor England even in quite humble cottages. It was done with a kind of coloured distemper on canvas stretched on a wooden frame. The pictures were often Biblical subjects painted by the painter-stainer and they made a remarkably fine wall covering. They were of course the tenants' property and were carried from house to house on removal. Perhaps this accounts for the fact that there are few examples left in the houses for which they were made, but there is still one in the Ancient House, Ipswich, on the wall of the staircase leading up to what was once the 'great chamber', where it was found behind the panelling. It was framed under glass to preserve the now brittle material but it is still possible to see the great figure of Hercules as the central theme of the painting. The cloth belonged to George Coppyn, the original owner of the house, and is mentioned in his will of 1578 as 'Stayned Clothes of Storeyes hanging aboute the great chamber over the hall'.

In the Tudor period this kind of painting was called 'waterwork' and it was often done on walls and ceilings, though paint applied direct to wall plaster was more expensive than painted cloths. The practice was popular in counties north of London, but examples are few and far between today. There is an interesting mural on an upper chamber wall at Synyards, Otham, Kent, a fifteenth-century yeoman's house (Fig 40). Here a dull ochre wall has faint figures of a lion and a dragon; the painting appears to have continued round the wall in a running design, but there are many gaps and its significance is now lost. Curiously, the medieval builder had a liking for ochre and not only painted his walls with it but often his timbers as well.

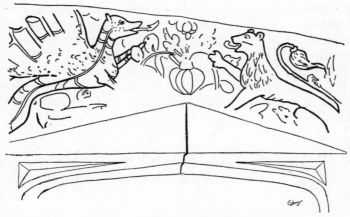

FIG 40   Wall painting, Synyards, Otham, Kent

Roof timbers and shutters also were often painted in bright colours. In the romance *Arthur of Little Britain*, walls and ceilings are described as being 'done with gold, azure and other fresh colours', in the style of the old Byzantine school. We know from other records of the use of gold or gilt as decoration and it may be that the many examples of dark red (red ochre) in existence are really the remains of the base or undercoat for this. A house at Newnham in Kent has the remains of a painting in a floral design on an ochre-coloured exterior wall.

Early in the 1950s alterations to the Bell Inn at Benington, Hertfordshire, opened up a capacious brick fireplace, spanned by an oak lintel 9in square, on which traces of a painted scene remained. The subject appeared to be a stag hunt, fragments of two deer, two hounds, and a hilly landscape being discernible. Suitable preservative measures were applied and this curious fragmentary painting remains as an object of antiquarian interest.

Painted cloths were probably the forerunner of wallpapers, though, surprisingly enough, the earliest English wallpaper dated from about 1509. It was based on the formalised damask pattern and art experts believe that it was probably introduced by a Fleming. One of the most interesting things about this first wallpaper is that it reproduces various materials, so that those who could not afford velvet or damask or leather could at least imitate them. Fine wallpapers have continued to be made in England ever since and all through the ages there have been attempts to copy the appearance of expensive textiles which proves that the old idea of the wall hanging remains in favour. The conclusion is that the timber-frame house is versatile enough to take almost any kind of decoration. It can be made to look gay or sombre—as the owner chooses, but it should never be lifted out of its period or it will lose all aesthetic appeal and its authenticity will be diminished.

NINE

Restoration

There is a Spanish proverb which runs: 'If one has a very bitter enemy the best way to revenge oneself is to give him an old house.' It depends entirely, of course, on the old house. If it is worthy of restoration and one has the imagination to penetrate through the clutter of years to the original fabric beneath, then it is a gift not to be despised.

Restoration requires an intelligent approach and much careful thought as well as energy and enthusiasm. With a house of any size or status its period and plan should be fully investigated before work is begun. Without knowing its architectural history it will be almost impossible to unmask its essential character and the main purpose of restoration will be lost. You must also know enough to be able to detect the genuine from the imitation, to know what to discard and what to retain; and the worst stumbling block here will probably be the work of a former restorer whose alterations and additions have disguised the original features, making the building difficult to date.

There is a modern method of dating timber by means of a radio carbon test which is based on the fact that all natural materials have a built-in radiation quality which, as soon as they 'die', escapes very slowly. By knowing as they do now what is the normal natural level of the radiation in the material, by measuring what is left, and knowing the rate at which it would normally disperse, scientists can work out the age as far as 'death' is concerned. It is an expensive process, but helpful in many cases.

A local archaeological society will usually be of the greatest practical help in dating a building, and in analysing its structure they also extract some of its hidden features. For example, a house at Aspenden, Hertfordshire, which was recorded by the East Herts

Archaeological Society, was obviously timber-framed though plaster
rendering concealed the fact from the casual observer. The house was
tall and broad, the main block having a gabled cross wing at each
end. Victorian bay windows and barge boards, superimposed on a
thorough eighteenth-century overhaul, left nothing visible of the
earlier work, but judged on general form the house was reasonably
supposed to have a seventeenth-century core. All uncertainty was
ended by a visit to the loft, where a blackened crown-post roof truss
declared it to be a late fifteenth-century hall house, heavily disguised.
The crown-post discovered, it was easy to trace the rest of the two-
bay hall, which had been vertically divided in two, one part providing a three-storeyed staircase hall, and the other, with an inserted
floor, two bedrooms above a room and passage. But there had been
more than one conversion in the hall, for the existing staircase was
unlikely to have been the first and the fireplace in the inserted
chimney stack was inconsistent with an early date. When restoration
work was begun in 1968 some structural timbers were found to be
decayed (they were made of a softer wood than oak, probably elm)
and the tie-beam and the arch braces of the crown-post truss,
hollowed and chamfered on the lower edge, had been sawn off at
each end to accommodate bedroom doors. More satisfactorily preserved were the carpenters' marks, prominently scored on the braces
of the roof timbers and repeated on the posts.

This example shows how rewarding an analytical survey can be,
emphasising the fact that a timber-frame building of any size that is
undergoing reconditioning should be properly examined from the
foundations upwards, first to determine its structural condition, and
second to find out its origin, the main difficulty being that much
evidence is hidden until work actually begins. The best method of
restoration is to observe and learn as you remove, and think carefully
before you replace. The way in which timbers are fastened together,
and the position of the principal posts, main beams, and girders
should be a guide to the original type of construction. Hidden
features may often be detected through the unusual thickness of a

partition wall, which may conceal a Tudor fireplace, a staircase wall, or hall screens; a wall that sounds hollow when tapped invariably pays for investigation; and the stripping down of wallpapers may reveal some painted murals or early panelling.

FIG 41   Restored cottage, King's Somborne, Hampshire

By and large, town houses have suffered more from 'modification' than those in rural areas. A succession of plumbers, hot-water engineers, gas fitters, and electricians have in turn cut away the fabric to complete their particular job and very often weakened the whole structure in so doing. For example, gas pipes, water pipes, and electric cables have to be laid well clear of the floorboards, and it has been found on occasion that the workman in question has either cut or drilled a passageway for his materials right through a beam vitally necessary for the safety of the building. He has conformed with the regulation to keep clear of the boards but in so doing has endangered the structure in other ways. This is the kind of common error that must be looked for and rectified, for it is essential for the structure of the house to be sound or the whole purpose of restoration will be

Modern timber-frame houses. Plate 37 (*above left*) 'Ufton', Oxted, Surrey (*Grove Homes*), Plate 38 (*above right*) local authority terraced house, Balham, London (*Quikbild*); Plate 39 (*below*) 'Chilcotin', West Clandon, Surrey (*F. W. Sunter, MRAIC*)

I

nullified. A house that has been a shop, a warehouse, or office before becoming a house again is often the most difficult to restore, but it can be done after a complete survey by a builder or architect experienced in this type of work.

Foundations
The condition of the foundations can sometimes be judged from the appearance of the walling, where cracks and bulges will betray uneven settlements. 'Tell tales' stuck over cracks will show if settlements are active—a slip of gummed paper, for instance, will tear apart in a few days if there is any movement of the walls—and in this case an architect should be consulted about the advisability of underpinning the building. Nevertheless, it must be borne in mind that there is usually a certain amount of movement in a timber-frame house. Excessive movement in the frame could be due to loose pegs in the joints caused by shrinkage over the years; this can be cured by knocking the pegs hard home or by replacing them with new slightly tapered pegs cut oversize for the hole.

Inspecting the timbers. We have already seen how the construction of an old roof can lead to the discovery of lost features, but other discoveries may not be so welcome. Quite often tie-beams are severed to make doorways or staircases, and if the restorer finds this has happened he should make good the beam without delay lest the walls bulge and the roof collapse for want of its support. The roof timbers should also be examined for signs of decay, especially at the feet of the rafters where trouble will cause the ridge to sag, also the joints between the rafters, and the ties and all other similar vulnerable points.

Structural timbers throughout the house should be just as carefully examined, especially the main sills and the feet of the main posts, where the grain end of the timber is susceptible to damp. Damage to beams by decay can be covered by a patch, but it must be done skilfully so that the new wood blends with the old. This is work for the trained craftsman, not the do-it-yourself enthusiast. There is usually plenty of thickness to old timbers, which allows a certain amount of repair work to be done with safety. Where beams have to be replaced in their entirety it is best to use salvaged material, which will match and be well seasoned for such restoration work; there are usually some to be found in the rural builders' yards, particularly after an old building has been demolished. The rural small builder is quite a collector of useful bits and pieces and he is also a mine of information on likely supplies from derelict buildings.

A great number of broad heavy beams were taken out of medieval houses when they were 'modernised' in the late seventeenth century. At that time floors and ceilings were given softwood joists spanning the room and the central beam was discarded. These salvaged beams can be recognised by slots at regular intervals along their sides where the floor joists were once housed. They are splendid timbers, still serviceable, and can be re-used by the restorer in a number of ways—replacing chimney beams, for instance, or strengthening weak places.

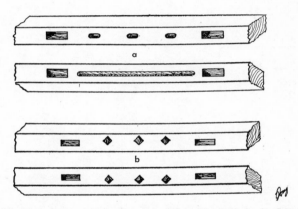

Fig 42   Mortises in timber indicating (a) wattle and daub, (b) mullioned window

Many people have been told that they have old ships' timbers in their home, part of the Tudor fleet which was broken up. It is a romantic idea, attractive to lovers of 'olde England', but it is hardly feasible; for ships' timbers would have been much too hard to work after years of soaking in salt water and in all probability they would have been the wrong shape for house beams. It is far more likely that many re-used timbers came from the abbeys and monasteries that were dissolved after the Reformation. It is still possible to find some of these authentic timbers today, and such finds will set the seal on a true restoration; they usually have a number of unexplained mortises on them for studs, mullions, or wattle and daub from their original use in other buildings (Fig 42).

During the dismantling of 'Bayleaf', a fifteenth-century yeoman's house at Bough Beech, Kent, a series of three long shallow mortises were discovered on the beam which carried the jettied first floor. At each end of these mortises was a shorter mortise, which might have held the tenon of a stud. The whole group was in the position of the front door, according to other local houses of similar style and period. By following the style of the chamfer between the outer mortises and noting the centre that had been scribed in the middle mortise it is possible to reconstruct the original two-piece Tudor doorhead (Fig 43).

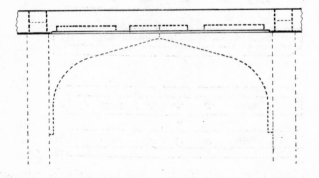

FIG 43　　Reconstructed arch

With all old timbers it is essential to make sure that the joints are secure, but at the same time they should never be forced back into position. The texture of English oak is moderately open and rather uneven, which makes it subject to distortion; and provided that the joints are safe, it is better to accept some irregularity, which is seen in all old timberwork, than to court disaster by unnecessary interference, and at the same time making restoration obvious. Oak also has a tendency to crack along the grain, which does no harm at all.

If the cracks are wide they can be caulked; but never fill them with cement, for it will ruin the appearance of the wood and provide a reservoir of damp in wet weather.

Damp

This is the worst enemy of an old building. It is important, therefore, to inspect all possible sources of trouble, such as broken roof tiles, leaky thatching, faulty flashing round chimneys or under window sills, cracked or broken water pipes and waste pipes, imperfect glazing, faulty or leaking damp-proof courses, and unventilated wooden floors.

The damp-proof course is a relatively modern innovation. Although a house may have survived for several hundred years without such protection, any alteration to its structure or a local upset altering the natural drainage would make it necessary. Even in large towns there are cases of dry buildings suddenly developing damp walls or flooded basements through nearby developments or demolitions upsetting the natural drainage over a wide area and even diverting long-forgotten underground streams.

The only cure for rising damp is the insertion of an efficient damp-proof course. Modern building regulations insist upon one in new buildings, but it is often lacking in old houses. The conventional type of damp-proof course usually consists of horizontal membranes of some non-absorbent material fixed well above the surface of the ground to prevent moisture being drawn up into the walls by capillary attraction. Air bricks may also be inserted at intervals to ventilate the space beneath the floor and to prevent dry rot. There are some more modern methods of damp-proofing on the market today but they are not all suitable for timber-frame houses.

In some houses it may be found that the ground floor is lower than the ground outside. In a small house the problem of damp can be overcome by the simple expedient of providing a very wide path round the house on a level with the ground sill, and making sure that it is properly drained.

It may be desirable to excavate the ground floor in those cottages with little more than 6ft headroom, bearing in mind that the new building regulations require a minimum of 7ft 6in room height in areas other than London where 8ft is the minimum height. The fact that some cottages have so little headroom may not be due so much to the popular supposition that our ancestors were shorter than we are as the fact that the cottages were originally a single bay, open to the roof, and when a dividing floor was put in it did not allow for enough headroom. When floors are up for inspection it is not a difficult matter to lower their level and so save a few cracked heads on beams.

It will sometimes be found that a restorer of a previous age has solved the problem in the upper storey by raising the height of the eaves and inserting a window in the gable, thus greatly improving the convenience of the bedrooms. This method is seen in some old houses in the Welsh Border counties, one at Castle Caereinion being a typical example. The modern restorer who copies these methods

FIG 44   Eaves of roof raised, Montgomeryshire

will then have ample opportunity to inspect for rot, which is likely to occur almost anywhere where dampness, stagnant air, and warmth are combined. Thus ill-ventilated places under floors, in roofs, or behind panelling are the main danger spots.

Dry Rot and Wet Rot
It is amazing how little attention is paid to preventing moisture from getting into timber and woodwork, for decay cannot take place in

dry wood. The term 'dry rot' is somewhat misleading as it only occurs in damp timber. Since it usually starts in damp unventilated corners that are hidden from view, it may not be detected until it has reached an advanced stage. When a house is being inspected it should be looked for automatically. Watch for any irregularities, such as crinkled or cracked surfaces of panelling, boards, or floorboards, and test any doubtful parts by inserting the sharp point of a pen-knife gently into the suspected wood; if dry rot is present the knife will meet with no resistance and the wood will crumble at its touch, but where the wood is healthy the tip of the knife will be gripped by the fibres, making it quite difficult to withdraw.

The dry rot fungus smells like toadstools, unmistakable in a place where the air is stagnant. It should not be confused with mildew, a superficial mould caused by damp, which does no more than dis-colour plaster or woodwork, and whose stains can be removed by brushing or planing. Mildew, however, does show that there is damp about, and as damp may lead to dry rot every effort should be made to dispel it.

Wet rot, by contrast, refers to the decay of timber under very wet conditions. It often shows little or no visible sign of growth on the surface of the wood, though there may be considerable cracking along the grain. It is found in very damp places, such as leaking roofs or cellars (see Chapter Ten).

Roof Covering

Where a roof is leaking badly it is better to strip it than patch it, since a patched old roof seldom functions efficiently. Old tiles and slates should be re-used for roofing wherever possible, for they are valuable. Where heavy stone is used the slates may need to be wired to the rafters with copper wire to prevent their weight causing any movement.

Thatching should be done by a skilled craftsman, not the village 'bodger'. The thatcher will judge whether a roof needs to be stripped down and entirely re-thatched or whether it can be repaired satis-factorily. Sometimes the only new part that is required is a ridge, the main body of the existing thatch needing to be cleaned down to remove moss and other growths and any worn places to be filled in. Any old wire netting which is taken off a roof should be replaced

with new, firmly fastened down. After the work is completed it is
advisable to engage the thatcher to make regular inspections, say
every two to three years.

In all cases, the original materials would probably have been of
local origin and it will be out of keeping to introduce anything
'foreign'; therefore the golden rule for restoration is to use salvaged
material or the same kind of material as the original.

Cladding

A timber-frame house, covered with plaster, hanging tiles or weatherboarding should not be affected by damp unless the outer skin is
broken; but exposed framing, without and within, having panels
filled with plaster or brick nogging, needs a little more care to
exclude the weather. The design of a house very often demands that
the old timbering should be visible both inside and out, as in some
of the old yeomen's houses we have already described. To cover such
framing would be a mistake but it does need some protection from
moisture. Providing each panel with vertical drainage in the form of
a groove in the oak will very often suffice, and will help to avoid the
formation of little pools of water on the tops of horizontal timbers.

In this context it is probable that much timber-framing exposed in
the past by over-enthusiastic restorers was originally clothed and for
a very good reason, therefore it may be advisable to plaster the wall
timbers within a room in order to keep out the draught. The plaster
should be applied on to split laths—sawn laths might well snap under
stress of the movement usually present in timber-frame buildings. In
areas where building regulations forbid the use of exposed timbering
on both sides (ie inside and out) it will be necessary to clothe either
an inner or an outer wall, because of fire risks, and the restorer will
have to choose one or the other.

Where existing plastering is showing signs of disintegrating it
should be completely stripped down and renewed. Lime plaster is
the only kind that should be used on an old building, and where
repair work is necessary the composition of the original should be
noted and copied as far as possible. The thick hair plaster we use
today had its origin in the sixteenth century when the Renaissance
builders used it for interior decoration. The chemistry of plaster,
however, is complex, requiring specialist knowledge; where any

elaborate restoration work is involved it is wise to call in a specialist firm.

Brickwork

The restoration of brickwork presents a different problem, for nearly all bricks made before about 130 years ago were hand made and are distinguishable by their texture. Their beauty lies in the fact that each one is different, with slight irregularities formed by creases in the making and variations in colour. A close look at a hand-made brick will reveal a variety of shades, but they all blend together in a very pleasing manner. Machine-made bricks never quite achieve this distinctive character, nor in the main are they so long-lasting. With hand-made bricks the clay is so soft when they are moulded that the finished products are solid and free from laminations. The only maintenance needed for a wall of hand-made bricks is pointing of the joints every ten years. The bricks themselves will mellow and improve with time and will not normally deteriorate; they seldom need replacing unless they have been lost or deliberately destroyed.

The texture of a brick wall or panel also depends upon the composite effect of brick and joint, distinguished by the technique of laying—ie Old English bond or Flemish bond. Alternatively, bricks were laid in what is now known as stretcher bond, the method used for building walls one brick thick, ie 4½in; the English and Flemish bonds were used in walls two or more bricks thick. Where brick panels are put in place of wattle and daub, the use of stretcher bond makes it possible to lay bricks without cutting them in half (Fig 45). For all methods the joints should be in lime mortar, the whitish or creamy tint emphasising by contrast the true colour of the brick. Cement or mortar of a darker colour would destroy the colour of the brickwork and look like an obvious patch. English bond may look better for fairly thick joints and a slight irregularity, but with Flemish bond regularity is important, with finer and more even joints to give a unified and balanced effect.

Some brick panelling, originally set flush, may have been plastered over at some time so that the panels project slightly beyond the lines of the timber, which appears to be sunk in the general surface of the building. This rather unusual feature should be carefully reproduced

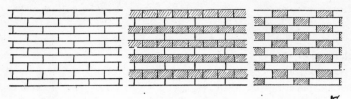

FIG 45   Brick bonds: stretcher, English, and Flemish

during restoration, unless, of course, you intend to return to what you know was the original appearance.

Where a tile-hung house is being reconditioned great care should be taken to preserve any original 'mathematical' tiles, which are very valuable nowadays. They will probably be about 250 years old, hand made, very tough and designed to look like brickwork; and practically impossible to replace without scouring old derelict buildings.

Windows

Occasionally it is desirable to add one or two windows to an old house, particularly if it is one that faces north with a comparatively windowless south wall. There are still a number of such houses in various parts of the country, probably because the early Elizabethans believed that the dreaded plague was borne on the south wind and they were afraid to let it into their houses. This absence of south windows is particularly noticeable in houses of the single-span type, for no good reason unless the builders were economising, but in any type of house it is not a difficult matter to insert new windows and introduce light from another aspect. It is easier in fact than it would be in a house of a later era and it will certainly mean a great improvement all round. At the same time, it will need some very careful research to keep the new windows in scale with the design of the building and to maintain a correct balance, for the appearance of a house can be ruined and its authenticity brought into dispute by the wrong type and size of windows.

Both window furniture and door furniture are highly important details which need careful study if a true picture of the period is to be presented, but the type of latch or fastener used varies with different regions. A County Museum will often supply this specialised information and will display the items that were used in its area throughout all periods so that they can be faithfully reproduced during restoration.

Wrought Ironwork

Many old houses possess some beautiful wrought-iron gates, balustrading, brackets, ornamental door hinges, and so on, which may well be the work of one of the seventeenth-century masters of the craft and should be properly restored at all costs. There is also plenty of inferior machine-made ironwork, probably replacing hand-made work, which is not worth renovating. It is helpful, therefore, to be able to distinguish between them.

In hand-forged work the ends of scrolls are individually treated either by tapering the metal down to the tip or by fashioning it into a leaf or other decorative forms known as snubs. The components are forged and fastened together into the finished article with the traditional use of rivets and collars but where two or more pieces branch from each other a gracefully blending 'flow in' is produced by hammering the metal together while it is hot enough to be malleable. In cheaper mass-produced work these signs are missing. The ends of scrolls have a chopped off appearance, and the component parts of a piece are welded by gas or electric-arc, and, if not properly cleaned up by grinding, are left with unsightly blemishes. Sometimes there is an obvious attempt to disguise an inferior piece of work by making hammer bruises to produce the effect of hand forging, but this is quite wrong, for the best wrought ironwork is free from disfigurement of any kind.

Some of the early designs were of exquisite delicacy—intricate repoussé work with embossed leaves, ribbed, veined and raised by hand forging with small hand-tools to produce a lifelike appearance. In restoring such work the craftsman has to be highly skilled, and there are few to equal the rural smith in this field. With fewer horses to shoe he has adapted himself so well to new sorts of work that many commissions for valuable restoration work now go to the country workshop in preference to the urban firm. The Council of Small Industries in Rural Areas will give advice in this respect.

Joinery

Any kind of old joinery is best taken down and sent to the workshop for repair, if funds permit, for it is usually well worth saving. Stairs are an important architectural feature and should be properly protected while restoration work is going on. The treads of an old staircase usually show signs of wear and may need to be strengthened from the underside, but if the framing itself is shaky the entire staircase should be taken down and repaired. Where this is impossible or impracticable the original feature should be reproduced by a craftsman.

Fireplaces

Fireplaces have usually suffered more often in the hands of 'improvers' than any other part of the house, and if the restorer wants to bring one back to its original form he should first make quite sure what that form was. Many timber-frame houses had at least one big open log-burning fireplace, though it might have been an addition to the original structure. As a rule it is simple to find out, because the mantel beam would scarcely have been disturbed; though it may well have been hidden behind a modern tiled fireplace which in turn has been superimposed on a Victorian grate.

Generally speaking, once the original fireplace is restored the problem of smoke control arises. Our forefathers had enormous fires and plenty of draught to keep them going, but even so they must have been resistant to smoke. Nowadays we find it better to confine the fire to an inner fireplace and channel the draught by a hood tapering well up into the flue. If you intend fitting a closed solid fuel unit, the simplest method is often to have a fireclay liner put right up the chimney, thus preserving outward appearances. It should be remembered that the use of any modern heating appliance in an old chimney will cause condensation, due to the products of combustion of certain fuels, mainly sulphuric acid, which will cause progressive deterioration of the brickwork and staining of the outer walls. This can only be cured by completely relining the flue.

Chimney Stacks

They need careful inspection to eliminate the danger of fire from faulty flues. The old stacks were built with wide bases to accommodate the huge fireplaces, and tapered like a pyramid as they reached the roof, but when later generations added fireplaces and new flues they often cut away part of the original structure without regard to safety. In repairing a stack it should also, if necessary, be restored to the scale of the house. It may be that a previous owner has raised the height in order to get rid of a downdraught, and the stack looks unwieldy and out of proportion. If you do not intend to use the fire, you can restore the stack to its former height, but this will entail some research into regional forms if the restoration is to be true to the original.

Modernisation

The hardiest enthusiast will scarcely want to forgo all modern comforts and will think in terms of central heating, up-to-date plumbing, and labour-saving kitchen quarters, all of which can be incorporated into the building during the initial upheaval of reconditioning.

As a rule central heating can be fixed quite unobtrusively, but as far as possible the run of the pipes should be kept away from old oak lest the dry heat causes the timber to warp and break its joints. There is also a danger that glued joinery will fall apart and it is as well to bear this in mind when placing pipes and radiators. Storage heaters will also dry the atmosphere, as will any other dry form of heating, but the installation of humidifiers will largely counter this effect. These problems do not normally arise in the modern form of timber-frame building, which is specifically designed to include this form of heating.

Electrical installations and wiring or the probable re-wiring of an existing circuit are worth the closest attention. Many a valuable house has gone up in flames as the result of a faulty electrical circuit. Oak contains tannic acid, which has a corrosive action on lead; lead-covered electric cable should never be fixed to oak beams, because of fire risk. Tannic acid also attacks iron, which means that any nails used in oak should be made of copper or be heavily galvanised.

Furniture and Furnishings

In restoring an old house we should not forget that the furniture and furnishings should be in period. Books on furnishings of the period and visits to museums such as the Victoria and Albert, London, will be of considerable help, but there are still some who prefer to consult the experts. Many firms of interior decorators run a specialist service of this kind and will gladly give advice, either by post or by personal call.

Conversions

The idea that medieval restoration will bring discomfort has been completely exploded by the many excellent conversions that have been successfully undertaken within the limitations imposed by law.

Tolleshunt D'Arcy Hall, which has been mentioned before, is listed as an ancient monument and is therefore protected by law, but it is a splendid example of faithful restoration and discreet modernisation by its present owners. It was a relatively simple matter to install small-bore oil-fired central heating, with the pipes running unobtrusively behind curtains and along skirtings. The boiler is concealed in a brick lean-to at the back of the house and the timber-framed eight-bay Tudor dog kennels on the edge of the moat now house the oil storage tanks, with a pipe running underground from the kennels to the house. Another main improvement was made on the first floor where part of one huge thoroughfare room, which served as a combined bathroom and WC (with no less than three doors), was turned into a corridor. Formerly, when the three doors of the thoroughfare room were locked no one could pass from one wing to the other unless they used the second staircase. Now this unwieldy bathroom has been carved up into a large bedroom and a walk-in linen cupboard, still leaving space enough for the corridor, while a new modern bathroom and a separate WC were built in place of the original linen cupboard. Thus all the upstairs rooms are now connected by corridors and privacy is assured.

Turning now to a smaller house, an architect restoring and modernising a fifteenth-century house in Horsham, Sussex, saw the potential advantages of the extensive space in the roof. With the judicious incorporation of two large roof lights and insulation material between the rafters, it made an ideal studio. He also installed central heating and to guard against heat loss in the principal rooms he removed the exterior wattle and daub panels and inserted some insulation material behind plaster. Some floors were lowered to give more headroom and a huge Elizabethan brick fireplace was restored to its former state. The kitchen was thoroughly modernised, but the walls were timber panelled in keeping with the exposed timbers in the rest of the house. In this way, a once decaying old house became a comfortable easily managed home of great charm and character. In addition, the owner had enjoyed the relaxation of building in the medieval idiom, recapturing the mood of those ancient craftsmen whose marks and symbols were his guidance.

Pring's Cottage at Halling, Kent (Fig 21), is an example of a house which looked shabby outside and even worse inside and was in imminent danger of demolition. An archaeologist saw through its apparent decay and was able to restore an extremely interesting fifteenth-century hall house. The open hall had been subdivided at a later date with a massive elm cross beam that bears the weight of the chamber floor, in remarkably good condition. At the time the floor was installed the central tie-beam was cut out and replaced with a collar under a shortened crown-post—a very delicate operation if the walls are not to bulge and the frame collapse under the outward thrust of the rafters.

Some of the original features found in Pring's Cottage included fine Tudor doors with typical arched heads, two mullioned windows with evidence of former rebated shutters, and a big open cottage fireplace with a bread oven at the side. The crown-post roof indicates, on examination, a hipped extension at one end, but this had been lost during the centuries and replaced by a small out-shut, or lean-to. The hip construction has been restored to give extra room in the upper storey and enabling a good-size modern kitchen to be built on the ground floor. An additional room was also built at the back of the house in keeping with the original structure. Indoor sanitation, with a bathroom and renewed wiring, have brought the amenities up to date and made a comfortable individual home from a near ruin.

Making two or three old cottages into a more commodious single one has now become fairly common practice and, where the basic construction is sound, it is a worthwhile proposition. Sometimes the conversion may turn out to be a reversion to the original style—the building may have begun life as a farmhouse and only later have been converted into cottages for farmworkers. Either way the result can

be highly successful, giving a house of as many or as few rooms as
are desirable.

Hunter's Cottage, Houghton, Hampshire (Plates 1 and 2), was
originally one single-bay cottage, which was extended at either end,
and later divided into three. The hall effect was lost in Tudor times
when the fireplace and chimney were built and the building divided
into two floors, all of which can be detected from the line of the roof
ridge and the evidence of the internal timbers. The middle cottage
was the original, probably of fifteenth-century origin, with those at
either end built on at a later date. A risk was taken in severing the
end tie-beam at one end of the original building in order to open up
the interior rooms, but a supporting wall was put up to strengthen
the main beam of the roof and the building remained as firm as ever.
One of the former wattle and daub panels of the original section,
divested of its mud and wattles but with the upright stakes remaining,
makes a novel room divider. All the ground floors were removed and
a damp course inserted, and while this was being done traces of the
original fire on the earth floor were found; but it was possible to
leave the upper floors as they were, with the very wide floorboards
intact. The staircase had to be sacrificed owing to the accumulation
of dirt and the consequent fear of dry rot, but a replica was made in
such perfect style that it is difficult to detect the substitution.
Plasterboard was taken down from all ceilings to expose the fine oak
beams and the Tudor fireplace was restored to the central portion of
the building. Where doors had to be renewed suitable seasoned oak
was used and new windows were also made in correct period style,
the local blacksmith restoring or reproducing all latches and hinges.
There had been no kitchen originally, the big main room with the
open fireplace having done duty as an all-purpose room in the past,
but there was space enough to build on new kitchen and utility
quarters in the form of an L-shaped wing. Here again care was taken
to use old materials and to see that the design was a continuation of
the former building. Re-thatching the whole of the roof completed
a house that is not only good to look at but is also good to live in.
The restoration and new building took about a year. The owners did
not attempt to make a formal garden, which would have been out of
keeping with the rural setting, but wisely left old trees where they
have stood for centuries, part of the natural landscape, and paths as

they were intended to be, following the footsteps of generations of men and women who have gone before.

In some parts of Hampshire a barn or a stable was an integral part of the house and it was no mean affair, though it was usually an addition to the original. It was built with timbers as stout as those of the farmhouse and thatched over. Now many people have found, to their satisfaction, that the one-time barn makes an ideal kitchen, much roomier and more adaptable than its modern equivalent. This was the case at Apple Tree Cottage, Quarley, a timber-frame wattle and daub house of medieval origin that had obviously passed through many phases during its long existence. Now it has been enlarged and converted into a delightful country home, the integral barn doing duty as a spacious up-to-date kitchen with modern wood-faced fitments in keeping with the general use of timber. In the upper storey there are some medieval carpenters' marks clearly visible on the beams of the original section. They are not in strict sequence, which seems to indicate some rearrangement in past times. During re-thatching, when the ancient rough roof construction was exposed, there were signs that the house had begun life as a single-bay dwelling open to the rafters, which were smoke blackened from a central fire. Traces of the original smoke shaft were discovered, lined with wattle and daub thickly coated with the black 'barnacles' of wood tar.

It is the glory of these old timber-frame buildings that, provided they are in the right setting, there is always room to expand one way or the other, and by following the construction of the timbers it is possible to see where previous owners have made alterations and additions.

In general, timber frames of sound English oak, skilfully jointed, tenoned and pegged together, defy the assaults of time. Carrying the weight of the superstructure on their stout posts they can with equal facility be expanded or modified without weakening their strength. Many of these traditional timber-frame houses are being rescued and used as homes once again, doing a useful job while adding to England's national building heritage.

The Law

As with other forms of building, restoration work of a certain type

K

is subject to building regulations and the intending restorer should make himself familiar with them.

As long ago as 1877 the public conscience was aroused by the wanton destruction of many of England's beautiful houses, with the result that William Morris, Philip Webb, John Ruskin and Sir Edward Burne-Jones founded the Society for the Protection of Ancient Buildings, whose function it is to advise owners and builders of the best methods to use in the preservation and restoration of old buildings. We are also greatly indebted to such societies as The Council for the Protection of Rural England, who have striven to see that we do not lose the best and most historic of our old buildings. To crown these efforts, there were some important changes made in the law by the Town and Country Planning Act 1968, which we shall now summarise.

The Law on Historic Buildings

If a building is scheduled as an ancient monument it is automatically protected by law and the owner or anyone else entitled to do work on it is legally bound to give three months' notice of such work or alteration to the Ministry of Public Building and Works, which primarily bears responsibility for all such buildings. If the work is carried out without permission the owner is liable to prosecution. Many of our old timber-frame manor houses come under this ministerial protection and as a result they are admirably preserved as far as possible in their original state, with necessary modernisation in keeping with the style of the building.

Many more houses, protected by being 'listed' as of special architectural or historic interest, come under the jurisdiction of the Ministry of Housing and Local Government or the Welsh Office. They include some quite small cottages if they have any architectural significance or have been associated with well known characters or events. Such listed buildings are protected from demolition and from alterations that would spoil their character.

All buildings built before 1700 which survive in anything like their original condition are automatically listed. Thereafter selection is necessary and a provisional graded list is issued to each local authority. On this basis a statutory list is compiled which makes all the buildings thereon legally subject to the provisions of the Act

(Town and Country Planning Act 1968). The statutory lists may be inspected at the National Monuments Record, Fielden House, Great College Street, London, SW1; the Welsh Office, Summit House, Windsor Place, Cardiff; or at the office of the relevant County Council, County Borough or County District Council. There is, therefore, every opportunity given for people to verify the status of their houses before carrying out any kind of work.

Under the old law it was necessary to give notice of the intention to alter or demolish a listed building and the local authority or the Minister then decided whether to make a 'Building Preservation Order'. Now, under the new Act, it is only necessary to get a 'listed building consent' from the local planning authority in a similar way to that for obtaining planning permission for building, but it is an offence to demolish or alter a listed building without consent and the penalty can be a fine of unlimited amount, up to twelve months' imprisonment, or both. If, however, alteration in the nature of development is proposed, specific planning permission is required which in this case will also count as listed building consent.

Before any demolition takes place, the application to do so must be advertised locally so that any amenity societies and members of the public have an opportunity to comment and their remarks are forwarded to the Minister.

A listed building is also protected from a careless owner: if he does not look after it the local authority may, with the Minister's consent, buy it compulsorily. If it is deliberately neglected in order to re-develop the site the local authority may be empowered to acquire the building at a price which excludes the value of the site for redevelopment. In this way our historic buildings are protected on all sides. It is only where the hierarchy itself decrees their destruction in the name of progress that the cause is lost.

Not all old timber-frame houses are listed, of course—the majority are not—but if the restoration required involves any structural alterations or improvements, it is still necessary to apply for planning permission from the local authority, giving full details of the work before it is begun. Some types of work can be done without such permission, but the wise house owner will find out exactly where he stands beforehand. The present Building Regulations apply throughout England and Wales with the exception of the Inner London

Boroughs, which are controlled by the London Building Acts. The regulations replaced the old building by-laws made by the local authorities, so controls are now standardised by government ruling, though it is still the responsibility of each local authority to enforce them. The average house owner is affected by these Building Regulations when he wants to install any sanitary or certain heating appliances, or make structural alterations, as previously mentioned.

Grants and Loans
Although listing does not give an owner an automatic right to a grant or loan for improving or maintaining a house, these are sometimes available both from central government funds and from local authorities. Government grants, as a rule, are limited to buildings of outstanding architectural or historical interest and the Minister is advised about their suitability by the Historic Buildings Council for England. Local authorities have greater scope and are not restricted to listed buildings, though they may give a 'house improvement grant' for improving or converting a listed building that is to be used as a dwelling. Concerned for old houses with a useful life ahead of them, the Housing Act 1969 introduced more generous assistance for those who want to improve and modernise such homes.

There are now three types of grant available through local councils: for conversion, for the provision of standard amenities, and for the overall benefit of houses in multiple occupation. The first two are more likely to apply to the average owner of an old timber-frame house, and providing he is the freeholder or holds a lease with at least five years unexpired, he is entitled to apply for a grant. He may have to produce a certificate from the Land Registry proving his ownership. Under these conditions, he may then approach the local council, giving a brief outline of the proposed work, and he will be given an application form. Where the scheme is very ambitious (as in a full-scale conversion) he may have to submit plans, specifications, and an estimate, in which case it is wise to seek professional advice. The premises will be inspected by a representative of the local authority before grant approval is given, and on no account should any work begin before this approval comes through or planning permission is given. These are two separate procedures.

The state of repair of a house is an important item to be considered when estimating the cost of any improvement scheme; even so, the grants are generous and the council may pay up to one half of the estimated cost of modernisation as approved by them.

The ambitious owner who has dreams of improving and enlarging his house should not forget that he is also increasing its rateable value at the same time, and if he is prudent he will enquire of his rating officer the amount by which his rates will increase should certain amenities be included.

As the restoration of old timber-frame buildings very often requires the services of specialist craftsmen, a list of names and addresses of professional organisations and trade associations is appended at the end of this book, which will help enquirers. Where an architect is concerned, the Royal Institute of British Architects will require as much detailed information as possible on the house—type, size, location, use, historical importance, and present condition—to allow them to choose a suitable man.

TEN

Preservation

It is a waste of time and money to restore a timber-frame building and then neglect to preserve it. Timber is one of the toughest and most durable building materials known to man, but it is a dead organic material and subject to attack from rot or pest if reasonable precautions are not taken.

All woods belong to one of two groups, hardwoods or softwoods. This subdivision is made not on the physical hardness or weight of the woods but on certain botanical elements. Thus, the hardwoods are the product of broad-leaved, or deciduous trees, such as the oak, the ash, the walnut, etc, and the softwoods come from the coniferous, or true evergreen trees, such as pine and fir which give us the various 'deals'. In the standing tree, some of the outer rings conduct the sap on which the tree nourishes itself and these active rings are known as the 'sapwood'. As the tree grows the sap conduction is taken over by new outer rings while the cells of the inner ones die and by certain chemical changes become the 'heartwood', which is far harder and more resistant to decay and insect attacks, but not so easy to work as sapwood. Many old building specifications stipulate 'heart of oak' for good houses, and the pegs for making fast the joints in the timbers were always of heartwood, as hard as iron. Another stipulation was for well-seasoned wood where the moisture content was reduced to a level that would keep it stable in all atmospheric conditions.

Starch and other carbohydrates remain in the sapwood cells for some time after the trees are felled and the cell walls, composed of cellulose and other constituents, attract certain insects, which feed on them. But a timber-frame building is not specially susceptible to attack, for all types of houses that have timber in door and window frames, floors and roof, are prone to attack if the circumstances are favourable.

The British Wood Preserving Association and the Timber Research and Development Association recommend preservative treatment for timber in certain vulnerable situations—where it is in contact with the ground or below damp-proof course level, where adequate ventilation cannot be provided, and, in special cases, in areas where fungal and insect attack is known to be prevalent.

Dry Rot and Wet Rot

Both are caused by wood-destroying fungi, the most virulent of which is the *Merulius lacrymans*, the true Dry Rot fungus. *Coniphora cerebella*, or Cellar fungus, as wet rot is sometimes called, is simpler to deal with, but it is important to be able to recognise the appearance and symptoms of both in order to eradicate them promptly.

When the Dry Rot fungus is growing actively in a damp place it produces white fluffy cotton-wool-like masses, or mycelium, like a silky sheet; but in a less humid atmosphere it will form a pearly grey felted skin, with occasional patches of bright colour. These develop tough, fleshy fruiting bodies, shaped rather like plates, which produce millions of microscopic spores, or fungus seeds, which disperse in the air over very large areas. If they fall on unprotected damp wood they will germinate, and in their turn eventually develop fruiting bodies and the whole process repeats itself. Sometimes these fructifications develop under floorboards and the spores will drift up through the cracks. They are easily blown about by air currents and will form a film of fine reddish-brown dust all over a room; this may well be one of the first signs of dry rot in a house.

The fungus will also penetrate brickwork and is capable of passing over inert substances such as stonework or metal or in fact almost any material in order to attack timber in the vicinity. It is possible, therefore, for dry rot to spread from cellar to attic, or from house to house, if it is not detected in time. Wood under attack has a typical dark brown colour, is deeply cracked across the grain, and is liable to split into small cubical pieces, almost in the manner of charred wood. It becomes very brittle and light in weight and, inevitably, loses its strength.

Wet rot is rather more insidious in that it often causes internal rotting in floorboards or joists, but where cracks form they may be covered by a skin of relatively sound wood.

In all fungal attacks eradication and repair are a matter of urgency, even taking precedence over the thorough drying out of the building. Some architectural knowledge is necessary when locating the cause of decay, for all rotten timbers must be cut out and burnt on site, with care taken to prevent spore dispersal. When cutting out the decayed wood a safety margin of at least 2ft beyond the bad portion is recommended. Infected plaster should also be cut out, with a safety margin of 1ft round the bad area. Any walls showing signs of infection should be thoroughly scraped and sterilised by heat (a high-powered blow lamp is best, but must be used with great care near dry timber) before being treated with an efficient fungicide. Any sound timber left in the vicinity should be liberally brushed or sprayed with a preservative, as should timber used for replacement if it has not already been impregnated with preservative under pressure at the timber yard. All dry rot repairs must be carried out thoroughly if there is to be no re-infection.

The treatment for wet rot is the same, but since it is less virulent than dry rot it is not necessary to sterilise the brickwork. It can often be checked by removing the source of dampness and by rapidly drying the whole house. The installation of a central heating system, combined with adequate ventilation, is the best method of preventing rot. In fact, with proper precautions there is no reason at all why old timber should ever be affected with this disease. The critics of old houses should bear in mind that dry rot is just as likely to occur in the wooden floors of a modern brick-built house as it is in an old timber-frame house if the proper safeguards are not observed; more likely, in fact, since even the first-floor timbers can be in contact with damp masonry.

Timber Pests
'Woodworm' is the grub or larva of the wood-destroying beetle and the small worm holes in timber are, with few exceptions, the exit or flight holes caused by the beetles boring their way out after they have fully matured. Although they are unsightly, the main importance of these holes is that they indicate the damage that is going on; but before taking remedial action it is necessary to identify the insect

responsible. There are three main types with which the average householder need be concerned and these are the Common Furniture Beetle (*Anobium punctatum*), the most common pest; the Death Watch Beetle (*Xestobium rufovillosum*); and the House Longhorn Beetle (*Hylotrupes bajulus*).

The Common Furniture Beetle is red to blackish brown in colour, from one-tenth to one-fifth of an inch long, with wings. The female lays eggs in grooves on the surface of wood, or where the grain has been torn up, and these eggs hatch out in a few weeks into crescent-shaped white grubs which, when fully grown, are about a quarter of an inch long. They then bore into the timber, feeding upon it and filling galleries with the characteristic fine sand-like dust that often accumulates in little heaps beneath infested wood. The grubs take from one to three years to develop, and then they come to the surface of the timber to pupate and bore small round exit holes about one-sixteenth of an inch in diameter, through which they fly. They emerge during spring and summer, when they crawl and fly about looking for suitable places in which to lay their eggs and so spread the area of infestation. They normally attack sapwood or softwoods, so heart of oak beams are immune from this particular pest.

They should be destroyed by a reliable insecticide applied from early spring to late summer, either brushed or sprayed on, and also injected into the flight holes to kill off any insects still in the timber. Where it is necessary to replace infested parts the new wood should be treated before it is used.

The Death Watch Beetle gets its rather grim name from the fact that it makes a clicking sound which was formerly thought to presage death. The superstition has gone but the popular name clings, with unnecessarily sinister implications; for this pest is in fact far more likely to be met with in the roof timbers of old churches than the average house, though it is as well to know its habits and characteristics in case of a chance meeting.

The beetle has a preference for hardwoods and those that are already in a state of decay are a favourite repository for the eggs. The insect measures from one-quarter to one-third of an inch in length, and is dark brown in colour with patches of short yellowish hairs that give it a mottled appearance. The larvae are curved white grubs over a quarter of an inch long and covered with long fine yellowish hairs. The life cycle is the same as that for the common furniture beetle, but the death watch beetle leaves a larger exit hole, about one-eighth of an inch in diameter. The presence of small pellets in the bore dust identify this beetle, but it is advisable for the infected timbers to be inspected by a competent entomologist, if possible, between April and June, which is the time when the beetles emerge. The surface dirt and bore dust should be scraped off the timbers before they are treated, and a vacuum cleaner used to remove all débris; then the appropriate insecticide should be brushed or sprayed on twice during the period April to June and also injected into the holes, and it is advisable to repeat this treatment for four consecutive years. An architect or builder should be called in to check whether any timbers have been weakened sufficiently to need replacing, and re-used wood, if showing the slightest damage, should be sterilised by heat or treated with insecticide. New oak heartwood does not normally need preservative treatment, but softwoods should be given at least surface coating, or treated by one of the absorption processes.

The House Longhorn Beetle arrived in England fairly recently, though it has long been known on the Continent and in South Africa, but since at present it is only found locally in Surrey and Hampshire, it gives little cause for alarm. In appearance it is somewhat flattened, about one-third of an inch to one inch in length, and brown or black in colour with patches of grey hairs on the wing covers. The larvae are straight and fleshy and may reach a length of $1\frac{1}{4}$in. In England the larval period may be anything up to eleven years, during which time the damage caused inside a timber may leave it little more than a shell. There is very little external evidence of this beetle, except sometimes a slight unevenness of the wood over the borings.

If the house longhorn beetle appears the householder is advised to call in the expert, who will know how to exterminate this pest by the latest scientific means. All timbers in infected areas should be treated.

Some of the preventive measures of the past had their drawbacks. For instance, one advocated the steeping of timber in lime water to prevent attack by worms, but this had the effect of hardening the wood considerably and making it difficult to work. Presumably the use of limewash in the Middle Ages had the same effect. Kyan's process for worm prevention was to impregnate the timber with corrosive sublimate, which made it brittle, a fault in the other direction. Nowadays there is a safe and certain remedy available for all cases of infestation. The British Wood Preserving Association, a scientific and professional body that sponsors research into the use of preservatives and fire retardants, offers a free advisory service on all problems connected with preservation and the fireproofing of timber. In addition, the leading manufacturers of proprietary brand insecticides and fungicides maintain advice bureaux where members of the public may seek expert advice by post or by personal call.

Many people treat timbers with an insecticide during restoration purely as a precaution, and in new timber-frame houses treatment is often carried out at the mill, by a system known as timborising whereby the sap is replaced by borax salts under pressure. This, or some other kind of chemical pre-treatment is completely effective against all hazards.

Western red cedar shingles are often given a preservative treatment before they are delivered to the site, but where this has not been done it is better to treat them before laying them; then the whole of each shingle is fully impregnated, whereas when they are laid it is only possible to treat them partially. Those which have not received preservative treatment should be treated during the first five years of their life and at five-yearly intervals afterwards. It is also advisable to give the pre-treated shingles a regular five-yearly treatment in case the weather has reduced the effectiveness of the preservative. With such care there is no reason why these shingles should not last for fifty years.

There are, of course, a great number of preservation processes available today. There are vacuum pressure impregnation with creosote, the water-borne type preservatives, diffusion treatments with boron compounds, and dipping and steeping treatments with tar-oil type preservatives and organic solvent wood preservatives, all of which are equally effective.

Apart from this purely chemical treatment, which was never meant to enhance the beauty of wood, badly neglected old timbers need cleaning. They may be encrusted with a hard deposit of dirt that will need a thorough scraping to remove it—a Dutch hoe was used to very good effect in one case—and where such drastic scraping is unnecessary an ordinary sanding will usually suffice. Once the rough surface is cleaned down a coat of linseed oil can be applied, which is the treatment most frequently recommended by architects. Some people use button polish or even boot polish as a finish; as one enthusiastic lady put it—'It gives the impression of having been caressed by loving hands over the centuries.' Be that as it may, the preservative quality of the boot polish would certainly do no harm to the timber.

Old timber flooring should also be preserved wherever possible, for there is no material to equal it for resiliency or warmth. Sanding will remove the surface dirt and bring a floor back to its proper level. Since wood is porous one must 'seal' the pores efficiently to prevent the penetration of dust. Traditional treatments, such as the dust-allaying oils, paste wax, or button polish, are not as effective as may be imagined, because oils hold the dirt and are impossible to clean, wax is too soft to give any lasting effect, and button polish, or shellac, which was the original floor seal, is apt to scratch easily and become stained. There are many proprietary brand floor sealers that give excellent and long-lasting results, but the timber must always be properly prepared before they are applied—ie all other polishes or sealers must be removed with an abrasive cleaner, leaving a perfectly clean surface. A modern floor sealer does not normally require further treatment, but if an additional polish is preferred a resin emulsion should be used and not a paste wax polish, which will make the surface far too slippery.

This preservative treatment is effective in both old and new houses, making floors not only easy to clean and resistant to wear but proof against pests. Where floors are properly cared for they will mature with age and look good long after other materials have outlived their purpose.

External Preservation
Externally, oak needs no special treatment; it will provide its own protective covering when it has been sufficiently exposed and 'weathered' and it will do this best if left alone. But few people in the past appear to have been content to leave their timbers alone, and ideas and methods of preserving exposed timbering varied with different regions. In the north of England and in the West Midlands it was the custom to coat the framing with tar (latterly black bitu-

minous paint) and to whitewash the plaster in startling contrast, producing the well known black and white 'magpie' look. Sometimes this seeking after effect was carried to the extreme by painting brick houses black and white, a subterfuge too obvious to be taken seriously. In East Anglia the style is equally distinctive though less dramatic, the framing painted a brownish red and the plaster coloured pink, blue, or green. In southern districts, as already mentioned, the timber-framing is often completely protected by a cladding of plaster, tiles or weatherboarding.

In preserving an old house it is best to follow the old methods as far as possible, at the same time taking full advantage of modern scientific discoveries. This advice applies particularly to external plasterwork, which may need protection from damp. It should be limewashed, the surface first being dry scraped to remove all old loose and flaking limewash then well scrubbed with a bristle brush. Where there is a history of dampness or mould growth the walls should be washed down with a chemical solution containing a mould inhibitor and this should be allowed to dry on the surface. Cracks and any other imperfections should be made good and allowed to dry before the new limewash is applied. Many of the modern colour-washes are water repellent, giving an additional protection to an exterior wall; and though certain pale colours may be acceptable for an exterior, interior plasterwork looks better in white. Where damp penetration is suspected a coat of anti-damp silicone compound applied to the walls before painting will often cure the trouble.

Painting

Certain very durable softwoods such as Western red cedar may be left untreated, as may some hardwoods like oak and elm, but they may be waterproofed by the use of a colourless liquid preparation, brushed on like paint, and this will help to preserve them. In the main, painting is the traditional way of protecting the exposed surfaces of softwood from moisture, abrasion, and dirt, and nothing else ever quite takes its place. In the Middle Ages ochre was used a good deal and there are still many traces of it to be seen in old houses, inside and out. It was the 'sil' of the Romans, obtained from compact earth or clay and coloured yellow, red, or brown from the combination of hydrated sesquioxide of iron. It was a useful, easily obtained pigment, one which had excellent preservative qualities, though the colour may not appeal to us today. From this ochre developed our modern idea of paint, whose basic composition is lead oxide applied through linseed oil, a water repellent as well as a preservative for timber, for no insect will lay its eggs on the painted surface of wood.

For complete protection against moisture all the surfaces of the wood should be painted, particularly the end grain, but first, careful preparation is important if the painting is to achieve its purpose. The basis of this preparation is that the woodwork, particularly outside, should be clean and dry. Wood that has never been painted should be rubbed down with sandpaper until smooth, and dusted off thoroughly before the application of a suitable primer. Previously painted wood should be cleaned off by scraping, removing all flaky paint in the process. A large surface may be cleaned with a blow-lamp, taking care not to get too close to the woodwork and keeping the lamp on the move to avoid blistering and burning, following closely with a paint scraper and allowing the scrapings to drop into a non-inflammable container. As an alternative to a blowlamp a coarse sanding disc attached to an electric drill base is effective, but for smaller areas a chemical stripper will suffice, using a broad stripping knife to scrape off the old paint to a smooth surface. All trace of the chemical should be washed off and the wood allowed to dry before work begins. Any bare timber must be primed before the new paint is put on. Full directions are usually supplied with each tin of paint, together with advice on the appropriate primer and under-coat to be used. The preparation, however, is the all-important factor for success.

White is the accepted colour for restoration paintwork, and it is available now in a number of tones. Though weatherboarding is often seen stained or even tarred in some areas, it looks much better painted white.

There is no reason why colours should not be used in the interior, in the kitchen or the bathroom, for example, which will have been modernised; and for these areas, where steam is likely to accumulate, there are some good anti-condensation paints, which also check mould and fungus growths.

Ironwork, particularly if it is hand wrought, should be painted black. The surface should be cleaned of dirt and grease and any traces of rust should be brushed off with a wire brush until the bare, clean metal is reached. Bituminous paint used to be the standard treatment for all ironwork, but it is best now to apply a rust-inhibiting undercoat and then a metallic preservative paint. There is a good opportunity to paint wrought ironwork when it is dismantled for restoration.

Iron casements in oak frames should be well painted before fixing, so that no part of the metal comes into contact with the corrosive influence of the tannic acid in oak. It is an advantage to put a layer of some substantial anti-corrosive material, such as Denso tape of a suitable width, between the casement and the frame, and this will form an adequate barrier between the two and give additional protection. Where there is a large gap between the frame and the casement a twist of the same anti-corrosive material can be inserted; it will also help to exclude draughts.

Today paint is not only a preservative for timber but in some forms can also protect it from fire. There are a number of fire-retardant paints and finishes which meet the requirements of the British Standards Institution. When exposed to fire they immediately form a dense insulating barrier which effectively restricts the spread of flame and prevents the heat from penetrating to the timber. Their welcome discovery removes the last lingering doubt about the advisability of building timber-frame houses in densely populated areas.

Timber also possesses a natural fire resistance of its own, in that it resists the penetration of heat into the body of the wood. It also resists those stresses which might cause cracking or buckling in other materials, such as concrete and steel, and it has a capacity to retain water to the extent of about four pints to a cubic foot of 'dry' wood. So much has been proved by controlled scientific experiment. In practice we can see that wood is slow burning by the length of time it takes to consume an ordinary log and the way in which it forms protective layers of charcoal on its surface, so the big, hard beams of an old building may smoulder but will rarely burn through. It has been proved that the strength of the timber left unburnt is unaffected except for a minute layer next to the charcoal line, and a post that has been partially burnt actually regains some strength as it cools.

In this way, as in a good many others, a good deal of old-fashioned prejudice arising from ignorance has been dispelled as a result of a new scientific approach to timber and a reappraisal of its natural properties. All aspects of the problem of preservation have found a satisfactory solution and the owner of a timber-frame house, old or new, is virtually free from worry on that score.

ELEVEN

Transplanting a House

Those who care about the preservation of our old timber-frame buildings must surely be heartened by the actions of those people who are refusing to submit to the inevitable 'march of progress' and moving their houses, timber by timber, to a safe area. There is nothing new in this idea. The archives of almost any historic town will usually produce one or more references to such removals. It was fairly common in the Middle Ages and would not have presented any great difficulties, other than transport, to the builders who were so adept at erecting this type of house. They simply took the timbers down in the reverse order to that in which they were put up and re-erected them somewhere else, probably quite a distance away.

Mr Salzman records the removal of a house from Wimbledon to Shere in Surrey in 1377. It was a hall with two chambers attached, roofed with tiles, and it was set up complete with partition walls. The previous year a great barn had been bought at Wimbledon for £8 and removed to Shere, where it was used for storing the king's hay. Such examples are repeated in succeeding ages in various parts of the country and it was apparently quite a normal procedure to transplant a house in this way.

The house need not always be dismantled in order to remove it. To quote Mr Salzman again—a house constructed like this, with all the timbers mortised and pegged into one another, formed so complete a unit that it could be moved as a whole, with pulleys and rollers, and he cites an ancient deed of 1520 which refers to just such a happening, enforcing the building regulations of that time.

The same method of removal has been adopted in modern times, though for different reasons. A few years ago a seventeenth-century two-storeyed and gabled timber-frame house, classified as of historic interest, was in the way of a new multiple store in High Street, Hereford, and it was decided to remove it bodily to another site in the Market Square, 300yd away, where it stood for eighteen months, pending building operations. In November 1966 it was moved back to its original site and incorporated into the new four-storey building. The house, which weighed some 40 tons, was first strengthened by internal timber braces before being jacked up on to a chassis and towed on tracks through the centre of the city to its ultimate destination; and once there it was jacked up to the first-floor level of the store.

The cost of this piece of modern commercial gimmickry was £10,000, and all it has succeeded in doing is to make this fine old black and white gabled house, with its traditional decoration of cusps and bracing, perch unhappily between two very modern shop premises where it looks like a doll's house. We may deplore the

FIG 46   Transplanted house, Hereford

choice of situation, but the fact remains that the removal operation was highly successful and the building was preserved in its original but now inaccessible form and it follows the idea of conservation which is the basis of all such efforts today.

The Hereford house is a beautiful building worth preserving, but in some towns buildings have been preserved for historical rather than aesthetic reasons. For example, Ledbury, in Herefordshire, had a row of medieval timber-frame houses, known as Butcher's Row, which stood in the centre of the High Street. There the butchers followed the custom of the times by doing their slaughtering in the street, a practice which became a great nuisance and highly offensive to the more enlightened Victorian townspeople, who bought the houses by public subscription and moved them to other sites. One ended up at the rear of No 14 High Street, and is now in a rather forgotten state. It is obvious from its position that it could not have been transported as a whole but must have been dismantled and re-erected to its original plan. Two others of similar plan are at the back of some private houses in Homend (Fig 17). While they are not prominently displayed, these three houses may still be seen by those who are interested in the origins of this historic and beautiful old town.

A form of snobbery, or social pride, sometimes played a part in the removal of houses from one site to another, especially when brick building became fashionable. There was a timber-frame house in the street named Dogpole at Shrewsbury which was built by Sir Francis Newport in the late sixteenth century. It was a good enough house according to the standards of the day but when Sir Francis's grandson was created Earl of Bradford in 1694 he decided that it was not good enough for a nobleman; so, two years later, he had it taken down and a brick-built mansion, now known as the Guildhall, put up in its place. In due course the old timber-frame house was re-erected on a site near the Castle, where it still stands. With the addition of some windows and some discreet modern improvements it is a great asset to the town.

Bridgnorth, Shropshire, also owes its unique Town Hall to the removal of a timbered building from another site. The original Town Hall was burnt down in 1646, during the Civil War, leaving nothing but the stone arches intact. During the Restoration the City Fathers had no money to spare for rebuilding, so they took a large and very substantial timber-framed barn from Much Wenlock and re-erected it on the old stone pillars. Now the Town Hall is one of the glories of Bridgnorth, a building which every tourist stops to wonder at and admire.

'Progress' has generally constituted the main threat to old timber-frame houses and today they are menaced from all sides—more particularly from the making of new roads and motorways, from urban development, and from new reservoirs flooding large areas of the countryside. As we have said, some hardy individuals have even moved their houses to safer areas, despite the cost.

One brave lady moved her house from Ware, Hertfordshire, to Norfolk on the do-it-yourself principle rather than see it demolished to clear the site for a relief road. Her house was one of the smallest remaining fifteenth-century hall houses in England, with a great brick chimney shaft inserted in the sixteenth century at the solar end of the hall. There was a six-light unglazed window high up in the north wall, with square mullions diagonally set, and traces of a similar window in the opposite wall, both of them rare survivals of early domestic architecture. The house was worth saving, and worth the arduous work of drafting a layout and labelling each part before the work of dismantling was put into the hands of experts. Now, on its new site in Wells, Norfolk, 100 miles away from Ware, the old house, fully restored and reconditioned, will continue its life and no doubt give much pleasure to the owner who saved it and the people who will be able to see it in the future.

One must, of course, consider the law before embarking on a project of this sort. First, it is necessary to get planning permission to re-erect a house on any site. The local by-laws should be studied for any possible pitfalls, but on the whole the building regulations concerning any kind of timber-frame house are considerably easier than they were a few years ago. Planning-wise it is no more difficult to re-erect an old timber-frame house than it is to put up a new one, the same conditions applying to both.

Once a site has been found, outline planning permission should be sought from the local authority and plans should be shown in full constructional detail for approval under the building regulations. One of the plans should also show accurately and in scale the position of the building in relation to the site and its boundaries, as the distance from the boundary can affect the materials used in the exterior cladding. Such a plan need not necessarily be submitted by an architect—a surveyor will help. As a broad guide, a building not more than 25ft high and 30ft by 25ft, provided that it is not more than 16ft from the boundaries, would normally be acceptable. A house with a thatched or wood-shingled roof must be 40ft from the boundary. There would probably have to be some relaxation of building regulations for the internal walls, but, depending upon the nature of the original material, they could be made to comply with the regulations with the addition of plasterboard lining. The ruling is that there must be a half-hour's fire resistance internally. Some roof timbers would have to be treated; the local authority cannot enforce preservation of timber, but if a house were moved from a known pest area they would quite rightly press for it.

The planning authority would inspect the building at all stages of re-erection. The appropriate departments would approve the laying on of public services, such as drains, but gas, water, and electricity should be applied for separately. An old house in need of restoration would greatly benefit by being dismantled and re-erected, for it would almost certainly be given new foundations, a damp-proof course, up-to-date sanitation, and a general overhaul of its timbers under the watchful eye of the local authority.

The mechanics of transplanting a house are not quite so formidable as they might seem at first sight, but the dismantling should not begin until a specialist architect has made detailed drawings of the whole house and notes of any outstanding or unusual features. Roman numerals on timbers may be indecipherable, and incorrect if second-hand timbers have been added, making them difficult for a modern builder to understand, so he usually devises his own code of serial numbers to correspond with a plan for re-erection. These numbers must be fixed to at least two faces of the timbers, and must be fixed firmly enough to withstand rough handling in dismantling and rebuilding, as well as the possible effects of the weather. They should also be easy to remove after the work has finished. Punched or engraved copper or aluminium strips, secured with one-inch copper panel pins might be used, but paint is not usually suitable.

Great care should be taken to dismantle a frame in the correct order to avoid damage. If it appears to be sound, the roof covering and any cladding, wiring, etc, should be removed first, leaving the frame to be dismantled last. Where there is any damage to the frame it must be borne in mind that the cladding or filling may be carrying a load so that a different approach may be needed, but where there is doubt, advice should be sought. Some of the more massive members, like tie-beams, may need extra mechanical assistance to lower them to the ground without damage. Tremendous manpower must have been required to haul them into position with ropes and pulleys in the first place. Now mobile cranes can be hired for heavy lifting.

On the whole, the job is not difficult, it all depends on a common-sense approach and planning. After all, this is about all that guided early rural builders who knew little of load-bearing calculations and often could not read or write.

The architect who directs operations will want to keep as much original material as possible intact for re-use, for it is valuable and part of the building's history. It is inevitable that some will be destroyed and every effort should be made to replace it with salvaged material from similar buildings.

It sometimes happens that a group of archaeologists or other interested people are keen to save an historic house purely for educational purposes, and it is here that we are indebted to the museums of buildings that are a fairly recent innovation in this country. Continental and Scandinavian countries have recognised this need for many years and have set up open-air museums of this type, some of them subsidised by the State, but England has been strangely backward in this respect, despite the fact that we are more richly endowed with beautiful architecture than any other country in Europe.

St Fagan's Folk Museum, near Cardiff, was formerly the only one of its kind in the United Kingdom. Happily this situation has now been remedied by the opening of the Avoncroft Museum of Buildings at Stoke Prior, Bromsgrove, Worcestershire, which is devoted to the preservation of timber-frame buildings. It was the first of its kind in England, having as its main objectives 'to draw attention to and to encourage interest in timber-frame buildings of historic and archi-tectural interest and by removal and reconstruction at Avoncroft, to

preserve representative examples which would otherwise be demolished and lost for ever'. It also gives advice on the restoration of
timber-frame buildings on their existing sites and, what is even more
valuable, has established a school of carpentry at Avoncroft to train
carpenters in the technique of ancient timber-frame construction and
the skills of restoration, co-operating with other organisations concerned with research into English architecture and the new scientific
methods of dating timber.

Such a museum is of great educational value, to historians,
students, schoolchildren, in fact anyone who is interested in the way
in which people lived in the past. In its completed form it will show
a medieval community with all types of timber-frame buildings,
including a fourteenth-century cruck hall (the earliest form of timber-
framing within the region), a village with a yeoman farm and pond,
a group of cottages, a dovecot, and a street of town houses.

The first house to be erected was a fifteenth-century merchant's
hall house that once stood in a street in Bromsgrove, Worcestershire.
It was about to be demolished in a road-widening scheme of 1962,
when it was rescued to form the nucleus of the Avoncroft Museum
of Buildings. During dismantling it was found to have a fine timber-
framed smoke shaft (Plate 8), which was lifted and taken away bodily
with the help of two mobile cranes. Smoke shaft and timbers were
stored at Avoncroft College for the next three years while the
reconstruction of the house was planned. Eventually planning permission was granted in 1964, but it was still another three years
before the house was finally erected, as nearly as possible to its
medieval plan. It was a major achievement, calling for highly
specialised knowledge and no little ingenuity, for the original house
had, over the centuries, been added to and altered many times and
its original framework was hidden from all but the practised eye. All
the unwanted additions had to be taken away before the essential
structure could be seen. Where timbers were broken it was sometimes
only possible to find the missing part by carefully matching up the
grain and any discrepancies in form and style could only be made
good after careful research into local usage.

A similar project to the Avoncroft Museum was launched some
time later at a 6,000 acre estate at West Dean, near Chichester,
Sussex, where the Weald and Downland Open Air Museum, con-

FIG 47   The Bromsgrove house, Avoncroft

sisting of houses, cottages, and farm and craft buildings from the region, promises to be of the utmost interest. Its aim is to create a representative collection of mainly thirteenth- to seventeenth-century Downland and Wealden buildings in a natural setting, and its first major acquisitions were two medieval farmhouses, known as Little Winkhurst and Winkhurst Farm, which were on the site of a new reservoir at Bough Beech in south-west Kent. Winkhurst Farm (Plate 30), dating probably from the first half of the fifteenth century, was the smaller of the two and was unlike the typical medieval farmhouse in having a hall of two bays, reduced to one bay in its upper part by the flooring over of the south bay to provide a solar chamber above. There was no cross passage and only a single doorway. So the original house had no service rooms, as we know them, which leads one to wonder if it was originally built as a farmhouse, or was it put up for some other purpose.

The house was dismantled and transported to Sussex, 70 miles away, where the timbers were stored until the new site was prepared. The frame was inspected and any necessary replacements made, after which it was re-erected with the help of a crane in a very short time. Much of the wattle infilling of the panels was done by a team of volunteers, many of them students, who thus gained valuable knowledge of medieval craftsmanship in a practical way.

The third building to be moved from Bough Beech was a fine

fifteenth-century yeoman's house of the Wealden type, known as 'Bayleaf' (Fig 48), which, as shown by the smoke-blackened timbers in the roof, had once had a hall open to the rafters, with a central fire. The roof was covered with hand-made burnt clay tiles hung on to the rafters with wooden pegs, and during dismantling as many of these were salvaged as possible, the builders sending them down a narrow wooden chute to a man waiting below to receive them. The roof in skeleton form was seen to be characteristically medieval, with no ridge piece but with the rafters half-lapped and pegged together at the top, their feet resting on the wall plate. Collars were mortised in about a third of the way down, with a central purlin underneath them running horizontally through the middle of the roof. The superb crown-post with beautiful braces needed special care in taking down, but the big brick-built central chimney stack—a later addition—was pulled down with a wire hawser and tractor as it was not part of the original building and was not to be re-erected.

FIG 48 'Bayleaf', Bough Beech, before removal

The history of the house gradually unfolded itself as the timbers were examined before being taken apart and marked with small metal tags—the twentieth-century equivalent of the medieval carpenters' marks. It became obvious, from the placing of various slots, that one or two of the original timbers had been used before in an earlier building and that some timbers were replacements at some time difficult to conjecture—all of which presented some posers to the research director of the project, Mr J. R. Armstrong, and Mr R. H. Wood, a surveyor whose main objective was to ensure that the building was re-erected in its original form according to the drawings which he made at every stage of the procedure.

Now, thanks to these dedicated people, 'Bayleaf' looks as it did when it was first built. This happy ending was achieved through the co-operation and generosity of the East Surrey Water Company, responsible for building the reservoir, and the archaeologists, architects, local authorities and others who are concerned to save historic old buildings for posterity. Museums of this kind may well be the answer to the problem of saving what is best of our old buildings, at the same time making way for progressive schemes which are necessary for the needs of a fast-growing population.

TWELVE

The Timber-frame House in the Twentieth Century

'The longer you can look back the further you can look forward', was one of Sir Winston Churchill's famous aphorisms, which, in one pithy sentence, sums up the aim of this book. We have had a long nostalgic look back to the past, but progress must come from looking forward and adapting ideas and techniques to suit a rapidly changing world. We cannot stand still—that is an impossibility—but we can salvage what is best from the old world and use it to advantage in the new. That is precisely what is happening in the field of timber-frame house building, where modern methods again prove the truth of the old adage that there is nothing new under the sun.

The transition stage from old to new methods was long and beset with prejudice and opposition from those who would have discarded timber with the ruthlessness of 'big business' at its worst.

Up to the beginning of the eighteenth century timber had been in almost universal use, acknowledged to be the only building material capable of resisting tension and bending and absorbing stress, but by the latter part of the same century, when the Industrial Revolution was making its impact, there was a departure from the ancient timber tradition to one based on the use of coal and iron. Brick-making became industrialised and thereafter practically all houses were built with mass-produced bricks; and, with the exception of the largest, with little or no style to commend them. The age of fine hand craftsmanship was temporarily extinguished and the timber-frame tradition was lost for a time, yet never quite killed; for apart from its continued use for workmen's cottages, a group of British emigrants had taken the method to North America and there, as in the Scandinavian countries, its development was unbroken. In fact, timber building proved to be so popular and practical that 90 per cent of the dwellings built there each year are now timber-framed, proof against the bitterest and fiercest weather these northern climes can produce. It was, therefore, particularly appropriate that these countries should help us to revive our own timber-frame tradition, Canada and parts of Scandinavia replacing the timber that once came from English oak forests.

In addition to exporting timber, the Canadian Government gave a boost to timber-frame building in Britain by erecting throughout the country demonstration houses designed to prove that the new techniques could produce strong dry permanent houses at a lower cost than their conventional-built prototypes. With all this it took a long time and much patient research by such bodies as the Timber Research and Development Association and the British Columbia Timber Frame Housing Group to break down the prejudice of the British against timber-built houses. In this respect we also owe a good deal to some of our more far-seeing business men, builders, and local authorities, who saw in timber-frame building the answer to a difficult housing situation, both in economy and in speedier building.

One of the pioneers of timber-frame building, to a system which he later called FrameForm (Plate 32), was James Riley, who, soon after World War II, had such confidence in this method that he tried exporting prefabricated timber houses to Canada, thereby winning a Government contract. Thereafter he was closely involved in the development and production of timber-building systems in Canada, and later adapted these North American techniques to suit the less predictable British climate, where off-site fabrication of components is so often more prudent and essential.

To many people the idea of prefabrication was at first disconcerting, reminiscent of the dreary uniform little 'prefabs' that were hurriedly put up after World War II to relieve the housing situation, and no doubt they also had memories of draughty army huts. But there is no comparison between post-war 'prefabs' and the timber-frame houses of this second Elizabethan period, which are built to last and provide the comfort of the age, as were their predecessors. The very nature of wood—its innate resilience—means that a timber-frame house will last as long, if not longer, than the conventionally built house of the same era. There is no need to stress the durability of timber-frame houses, the survivors from the past are sufficient proof of that; the brick and stone filling crumbles but the timber weathers on. In short, the properties of timber never change, but the methods of working it and the species used must of necessity change with the demands of each new generation.

Industrialised Building

This has been defined by a leading architect as 'the integration of demand, design, manufacture and construction'. The modern timber-frame technique, though industrialised, still allows that essential freedom of design which the average architect and house owner desire.

There are two ways of building a timber-frame house nowadays: (1) by comprehensive system building, using a fully industrialised technique, or (2) by on-site fabrication of components using machine-prepared timbers.

Firms with factory plants and facilities have speeded up the process to such an extent that a terrace of three houses can be completed in seven days; and even small builders can complete timber-frame houses in three months or less, compared with a minimum of nine months when using the traditional methods. Taking into account Britain's shortage of labour and precarious economic situation, this is a vast improvement on all counts.

Choice of Site

A level building plot is, of course, the wisest and most economical proposition, but at the same time a split-level site presents no problems to timber-frame building. The lightness and strength of the frame makes it ideal for difficult sites and the general flexibility of timber allows it to cope with unexpected stresses and strains more easily than any other material. The ideal building plot for any type of house should have dry and porous soil, with the ground falling in all directions to facilitate drainage. There should also be free circulation of air in the area and any undrained ground should not be close enough for the prevailing winds to blow damp exhalations over the house. In theory, these are the ideal site conditions, but in practice these combined qualities are rarely found, and timber-frame building is generally more accommodating to those which fall short of the ideal than any other kind of building.

The decision between building entirely on site or having a house assembled from factory-prepared components may depend upon a number of factors: on whether there are builders available with sufficient experience of timber-framing to manufacture components, on what kind of accommodation is required, or on the cost, though timber building is flexible enough to enable anyone to build on a small scale and make additions later. Nevertheless, with the continuing rise in labour costs and the shortage of skilled craftsmen it follows that mechanised factory preparation is more economical in the long run. The leading manufacturers in Britain produce their components to strict and detailed specifications based on solid scientific principles. In general, the manufacturer provides the house in sections ready for quick assembly according to detailed drawings and instructions, but the actual work of building is delegated to a builder of his or the client's choice.

Some builders have their own factories and combine all functions into a package deal, designing, manufacturing, and erecting. This system is flexible, allowing the client either to have the whole job done for him or substitute his own design or labour facilities, at the same time drawing on the manufacturer's experience.

Main Types of Construction

Modern methods follow the stud-framing principle, using either balloon or platform framing. The timbers will probably come as pre-cut and accurately machined members, straight from the saw mill, or they may be complete components—panels assembled in jigs, roofs, floor decks, door frames with doors, glazed or unglazed window frames, and partitions with fixtures and fittings already attached. In other words, the whole process has become industrialised; the machine has superseded the house wright with his axe, his adze, and his scribing tools.

So, too, the methods of building up the frame components are vastly different from those of the old-time builder. Mortises, tenons and wooden pegs have been replaced by rust-proofed nails, screws, glue, and various metal-connecting devices. The wattle and daub and other old types of infilling have given way to scientifically designed wall claddings and linings which cover the structural timbers in accordance with Building Regulations.

The constructional stages in the erection of a balloon-frame house are as follows. After an inspection of the site, which may include boring holes to ascertain the nature of the ground and the composition of the subsoil, the foundations are laid. Unless local conditions demand a special treatment (such as a reinforced concrete raft) they are of the conventional type and ground floors may be either solid or suspended.

When the foundations are complete and the sill plates fixed the prefabricated timber frames are placed ready for erection. The front walls or flank walls, or both, are load-bearing, built up from timber studs spaced about 16–24in, assembled with plywood sheathing into firm unyielding panels of great strength though light in weight. Once

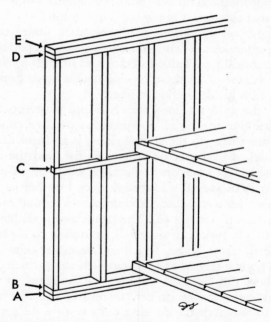

Fig 49 Balloon frame construction: (a) ground sill, (b) sole plate, ribbon, (d) wall plate, (e) head binder

the external and party wall frames have been erected and fixed to the ground sill and each other, the floor joists are inserted, the first-floor joists being fixed to the ribbon which is nailed to the studs (see Fig 49). Then the roof trusses are fitted to complete the carcass of the house. The roof trusses are laid on the head binder, which runs the length of the building on top of the wall components and ties them together. On the second day, the external cladding can be applied to the walls and the roof covering put on, so that the house is kept dry and weatherproof henceforward. When all services have been installed and the flooring completed the internal lining and partitioning are put in and the building is completed in record time.

One of the greatest advantages of industrialised building this way is that a house is virtually dry built, with all the traditional 'wet' trades, such as wet plastering of walls and ceilings, eliminated. About 1,250 gallons of water are used in building the average conventional house, but industrialised timber-frame building uses only about one-sixteenth of that amount. A house is roofed within forty-eight hours, and thenceforth all operations can take place under cover. The advantages are obvious. There is no long drying-out period, nor any 'settling', when walls are liable to crack and timbers to shrink. The householder is free of all these routine maintenance problems and can proceed with his decorating at once.

Internally, the walls are lined with half-inch plasterboard, behind which is a vapour barrier of polythene to counter condensation. Behind the polythene, in the stud cavities, is an insulating quilt of glass fibre backed by paper or other material, and the backing is stapled to the studs to keep it in place. On external walls there is a moisture barrier of special waterproof black breather paper, which covers the ply sheath and allows the timber—a natural material—to 'breathe' through it (see Fig 50). The final exterior cladding may be any one of a wide variety of materials, according to choice.

In a platform frame house, which can be rather more flexible in design, each floor is treated as a separate structure, which means that shorter timbers can be used—easing the problems of transport, handling, and selection of timber. Instead of the first-floor joists being fixed to the studs the decking units rest on the ground-floor components, the first-floor wall components resting on the decking.

It is, of course, possible to build houses, maisonettes or flats of any

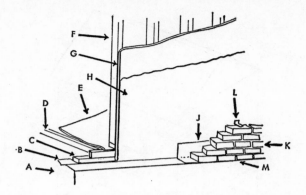

FIG 50   Frame cladding: (a) foundation, (b) damp-proof course,
(c) ground sill, (d) ground floor frame, (e) floor decking, (f) stud, (g)
ply-sheathing, (h) breather paper, (j) metal flashing, (k) brick-cladding,
(l) flexible brick tie, (m) weep-hole.

length and breadth and up to four or five storeys in height in this
way, and to have them individually designed by an architect, using
standard or slightly modified components. There are two blocks of
four-storey maisonettes in Wooburn Green, High Wycombe, Buckinghamshire, known as the Glory Hill Estate, which were designed
by TRADA and built for the local authority in 1966; they are the first
of their kind in the world built in direct competition with traditional
methods.

Timber has always been favoured by the architect because it
allows for flexibility in planning and takes a variety of elevational
treatments without difficulty. A modern timber-frame house can
look just like a conventionally built brick house (Plate 38), or be an
unconventional building using all the newest ideas and materials. We
have seen a compact bungalow, clad with brick, with two bedrooms,
a living-room, kitchen, and bathroom built on an area of 640 sq ft.
Because it is a modular house extensions are likely to be easy; an
extra room or two can be built on to it or it could be made into a
two-storey house. Delivered in component form, ready for assembly
by approved builders, this kind of house can be erected within a
matter of two weeks. It is ideal for local authorities, the design being

M

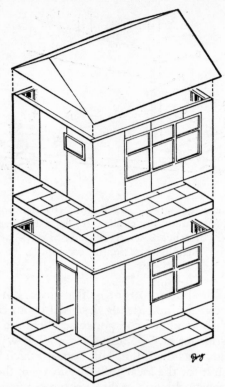

FIG 51   Platform construction

adaptable both for large housing projects and for filling the odd available site.

At the other end of the scale, there is a timber-frame house in North London which is so unusual that it almost has the character of a tree-top hide. It is raised on slender steel tubes so that the windows literally have a birds'-eye view up among the trees, with the space below taken up by twin garages. An inner living-room is partially enclosed, and there is an open fire at the very heart of the house. Around this main feature are grouped an L-shaped living area, a study, a hall, a bathroom, a large bedroom and bathroom en suite, and a kitchen. A sliding floor-to-ceiling window in the living-room opens on to an extra deep balcony that has been likened to a boat-deck promenade, and the balcony shelters an open paved area beneath the house—ideal for children's play. The playground and the garden are reached by a shallow stairway from the balcony.

This highly individual plan illustrates the adaptability of timber. Another instance of adaptability is shown in a business executive's house in Camberley. This house, a timber-frame Canadian-type home, was built in three stages, the first two to accommodate a growing family and the final stage to give a grandmother a built-on home of her own. At each stage extensions were added, the timbers, the white shipboard cladding, and the windows being repeated, so that it is impossible to see where the original house began and ended. In fact, modern timber-frame building invites experiments.

It is equally possible to reproduce old styles of building, suitably up-dated to suit the requirements of the owner. One such house is 'Chilcotin' at West Clandon, Surrey, which has been built as a modernised Colonial-style mansion (Plate 39) reminiscent of North American period houses. It has a white weatherboard and brick-clad frontage with a semi-open plan interior. The rear is more modern in appearance, with large windows and a projecting balcony at first-floor level. It is roofed with Western red cedar shakes, which are similar to shingles but thicker than the modern shingle, tapering from $1\frac{1}{2}$ to $\frac{1}{2}$in in thickness; they are not much used here but very popular in North America. They are laid on the roof so that there is at least three thicknesses of timber at any given point, and have a longer life than shingles.

As the medieval builders knew well, timber is an ideal medium for providing a jetty and this is a feature of many a twentieth-century timber-frame building, either to project the rooms or to form a balcony. A house at Oxted, Surrey (Plate 37), follows this design: half the upper storey is clad in vertical white timber shiplap and cantilevered to provide a balcony, thus relieving the conventionality of an otherwise plain brick-clad house. Another unusual circumstance about this building is that the kitchen and day rooms are on the first floor, whereas the bedrooms are on the ground floor.

Roofing

A most important part of any house, old or new, is the roof. Unless that is sound and well built the rest of the building will soon suffer. This elementary fact applies particularly to timber-frame building and it is one which has been given much thought and scientific research by the developers of industrialised building. Broadly speaking, the roof of the modern timber-frame house is built up from standard prefabricated trusses made mostly of Douglas fir, and as specified by TRADA. These trusses, which now replace the conventional purlin and rafter roof, are set at regular intervals, and where the pitch is very shallow, whether it be dual or mono-pitch, the rafters are usually sheathed with plywood to take the built-up roof finish, which may include shingles, slates, or concrete or clay tiles. For flat-roof construction the roof joists need a plywood decking to take the selected finish, which may be any one of a variety of proprietary materials. In its simplest form it can be a three-layer bituminous felt topped with granite chippings or felt and metal laminates, or even sheet metal. Metal coverings are made previously glued to strawboard panels. Aluminium alloy sheets are available in the form of roll-on and lay-on interlocking sheets. Some architects like copper because it weathers to a greeny-bronze and blends well with any landscape. It looks best on a mono-pitch roof with a fairly steep pitch to give it a sweep downwards. It is usual to insulate immediately beneath a metal covering to prevent condensation. Again, there is a wide choice in roof covering, ranging between the conventional red tiles and these more dramatic sheet metals, but before going in for the more exotic and unusual materials the house owner should make sure of its standard of performance.

In all cases the roof space is lined with a mineral or glass-fibre quilt for heat insulation, plus a vapour barrier, the ceiling then being finished with plasterboard. As an alternative, but a more expensive one, the ceiling may be clad with timber, such as untreated pine boards or Western red cedar, which can be treated to last for an indefinite time. In a ranch-type house, this kind of wooden ceiling looks particularly attractive, and is, of course, an excellent insulator in itself.

Flooring
It is well known that the resilient nature of wood makes it less tiring for the feet than less yielding materials and this, coupled with its

natural warmth, makes it the ideal flooring, particularly for children. Nowadays there are hundreds of woods available and choice of type is normally limited only by the conditions in which it is to be used, ie whether a waterproof concrete subfloor is to be laid, and so on, so correct specification and construction are just as important as maintenance.

The construction of floors in general includes joists (usually specified as hemlock or Douglas fir) set at regular spaces to take either tongued and grooved softwood boards, or $\frac{5}{8}$in tongued and grooved plywood, which are interlocked with tight draught-proof joints. Many builders using the new industrialised techniques prefer plywood flooring because of the speed in fixing. Plywood decking is very light to tread upon but is also tremendously strong and has proved to be satisfactory in every way.

For those who prefer hardwood block or ship flooring, particularly for the ground-floor living-rooms, there are a number of woods available and they look well in any setting. For example, Canadian maple, afrormosia, afzelia, makore, West African teak, and oak all are hard wearing and beautiful to look at, and the use of a recommended sealer will keep them in good condition for an indefinite time.

There are other, less conventional, flooring materials, though some are more expensive. There is marble, for instance, a beautiful traditional material that is again coming into more general use to give a luxury touch to an entrance hall, a cloakroom, or a bathroom; it is also very suitable for a dining-room because it is hard wearing and clean. The genuine quarried marble is only slightly more expensive than synthetic substitutes.

Slate is also used for flooring in the form of non-slip tiles. It is a good, solid material that can be worked with precision and keeps its texture and colour under all conditions.

Ceramic tiles are also highly effective in the right setting, the latest designs being very decorative and bright, dispelling for ever the old idea of uniform black and white.

Cork has gained steadily in popularity over the years. It is warm and easy on the feet and can be polished without becoming slippery.

Modern composition floorings come in a variety of guises, some good, some indifferent, and great care should be taken in choosing them. All need a recommended sealer to keep them clean.

The modern house owner, therefore, has a very wide choice and the timber-frame house need by no means be restricted to timber. Whatever material is used, a floor should have a properly prepared base, the preparation varying according to the nature of that material.

Cladding and Lining

There have probably been more technological advances in cladding than in any other field, giving us a variety of synthetic materials which at least vary the appearance of our buildings if they do little to enhance their beauty. Many of these scientific discoveries are good, but others have yet to prove their worth.

The most significant changes came about in early post-war days when it was imperative to use wood as economically as possible. The need for new materials intensified the search for timber substitutes and it was discovered that wood waste such as sawdust, chips, and shavings, having good insulation properties, could be converted into wallboards, straw into strawboards, and other cellulose wastes into fibreboards, all of which made good material for lining interior walls and ceilings. This gradual change from natural to 'man-made' timber has led to a spectacular advance in the use of board materials generally.

There is also a tendency to use more laminated timber, which is built up in layers with the grain of each layer running in the same direction. When bonded together with synthetic resin cements the layers make a tremendously strong beam that will take the greatest possible strain in the direction of the grain. It can be used to great effect in large post and span buildings. The sizes of straight laminated members have now been standardised by the British Woodwork Manufacturers Association, a fact which may increase its use still further, particularly in multi-storey buildings, where rigid construction is of the greatest importance.

Plywood, on the other hand, is a 'sandwich' of woods, consisting of an odd number of layers—three or five, for example—with the grain of each at right-angles to its neighbour. The layers are bonded together and glued with synthetic adhesives that are stronger than the wood itself and, where this is necessary, made completely waterproof. Plywood is so strong that it was used for the fuselages of some of the fighter aircraft of World War II, and is used for yachts and motor-boats today. With the use of modern machines and presses and synthetic waterproof glues plywood has been given a tensile strength almost comparable with steel. In timber-frame structures it has come to be used more and more in fabricated components, and as a membrane material in panels. In fact, it is used at almost every stage of building, and large plywood panels, scarf-jointed from standard size components, are now in regular use.

Chipboard and plywood are often veneered with rarer and more exotic woods to make distinctive linings or one-wall features. There is now a great variety of beautifully marked rare woods on the market, some of which were unknown to any but the expert fifty years ago; in the main they look their best in veneer form. For example, a modern timber-frame house in Kent has one long wall of gaboon ply (which resembles mahogany) in the living-room, one in Surrey has wall panels of rare East African nkoba and podo, while another, in Middlesex, has pear-wood-panelled walls that are a constant source of admiration. One could go on citing instances of the discriminating use of these distinctive woods, and in all cases they have added a rich, satisfying background to the general décor. A plastic veneer is also obtainable but it does not have the aesthetic appeal of natural timber.

Some people prefer to use planks of natural timber for interior panelling in the form of hardwood strips, or knotty pine or cedar used horizontally or vertically. Ceilings and walls can be treated alike, adding to the general warmth and comfort of a timber house, and in a kitchen or bathroom a warm surface reduces condensation. Pine is most popular here for it can be left untreated.

Of course, timber lining in any form is more expensive than painting or wallpapering, but once in place, with reasonable care, it will last for the lifetime of the house. Given a free hand, architects and interior designers will generally use timber lavishly, appreciating the visual quality of wood in emphasising the line and form of their design.

The final exterior cladding of a modern timber-frame house may vary from the traditional brick or stone to the latest composite materials, some of which are applied at the factory and others on site.

Sometimes a single skin of brick, tied to the timber with flexible brick ties, is used to give the house a conventional appearance, masking the timber-frame structure beneath it. The bricks may be the usual red, or they may be buff or charcoal grey Uxbridge flints by way of variation. Tile-hanging is another variation on an old theme, but for the less conventionally minded there are the new laminated plastics, applied as panels in varying bright colours; asbestos boards and composites, some of which have deeply ridged surface textures; and metals such as aluminium, copper, or stainless steel, vitreous enamelled and colour-coated, impervious to weather conditions and pollution. Some of the latest developments in cladding include panels of unglazed ceramic tiles or mosaics, glazed asbestos shingles, and frost-proof glazed tiles, all in a great variety of colours, with a matt or gloss finish. Decorative glass panels also look attractive, made up as they are of coloured slabs fixed in concrete or resin, and giving the effect of a modern stained-glass window.

There is a sheet-cladding material that resembles stucco, having a surface of crystalline stone chippings that are self-cleaning and entirely resistant to frost, damp, and corrosion. It also comes in a smooth form.

Strangely enough, this seeking for new methods of cladding has led the designers almost full circle back to the old ways of tile-hanging, cedar shingles and weatherboarding, but with modern variations.

When timber-frame building was revived in the first quarter of this century, the exterior surface treatment of ordinary softwood timbers was creosote. The first houses built were nearly always weatherboarded, with a liberal coating of creosote, like a model cottage at Merrow Green, Surrey, which was built in 1914, and the many single-storey buildings dotted around Hampshire. Creosote was practical and an excellent preservative, but somewhat undecorative, and we have since learned to make timber look more attractive without sacrificing any of its safeguards. White-painted weatherboarding cannot be bettered, it recalls old styles in a simple pleasant manner (Plate 39), but with the increase of road traffic everywhere and the consequent spread of dust and grime it needs more regular maintenance than many people are prepared to give it.

Therefore plastic-faced plywoods have been developed to look like timber shiplap, but not requiring the same maintenance. They are ready made up in cladding profiles that interlock horizontally and fasten with concealed metal cleats. Other versions of this simulated weatherboarding come in PVC, asbestos cement (grey unless painted), and aluminium. The last-mentioned is made in preformed sections with a weathertight overlap and finished with stoved-on paint to make it completely weatherproof. These claddings will not rust or warp and need only a periodic wash down with a hose or with soap and water applied by hand. PVC needs no maintenance at all since it is completely proof against rot, corrosion, and all weather conditions. Many of these surfaces scratch easily and should be carefully cleaned with plenty of water.

Despite all these attractive attributes of man-made materials, many architects prefer timber for cladding.

Western red cedar is probably one of the best known of the woods used, popular because it is so durable, needs no preservative treatment, and weathers well from a reddish brown to a silvery grey. *Californian redwood* is in the same category, weathering from dark red to brown. *Elm* is another favourite weatherboarding material, looking particularly attractive on a country cottage, with its wavy-edged boards weathering from dark brown to silvery grey. *Larch* is a similar durable wood, though its initial colour is more of a golden brown, and *oak*, still first favourite, varies from yellowish to dark brown at first and often weathers to a greyish brown.

Teak and *iroko* are used a good deal nowadays and are respected for their durability and weather resistance. Both are light brown when cut, weathering to a much darker colour. *European redwood* (*red pine* in Scotland), *Columbian pine*, and *Western hemlock* are also used on exteriors, but because they need preservative treatment they are seldom seen in their natural weathered state.

There are many bodies which give advice on different aspects of timber-frame housing. The Timber Trade Federation either deals with queries direct or passes them to one of the specialised organisations.

Insulation Value

In these days of soaring costs the natural insulation value of timber can save money. To quote a leading authority: 'For equivalent thickness, the thermal insulation value of wood is 16 times better than that of standard concrete, 400 times better than steel and 1600 times better than aluminium.' In addition, resin-bonded glass fibre and foamed plastics in the form of slabs have vastly improved the thermal insulation of walls and ceilings, so the well-insulated stud-frame walls of a timber-frame house keep it warm in winter and cool in summer. It is now usual to install central heating during building and the timbers are specially seasoned to withstand this form of heating without warping. Central heating in the well-insulated timber house costs much less than it does in the traditional house. Where double-glazed windows are included there is still more saving, because heat is retained more easily, and plumbing is better protected, reducing the danger of frozen pipes in winter virtually to zero.

Sound insulation is also a good deal better, and noise, which is becoming an increasing problem everywhere, is greatly reduced. Timber-frame party walls with $1\frac{1}{4}$in plasterboard linings and an insulating blanket in each stud cavity show average reductions of 56 decibels under field test. With this insulating barrier the noise from neighbours, road traffic, and passing aeroplanes becomes more bearable, if not entirely eliminated.

Timber-framing and the Local Authority

Although houses built with on-site or factory-constructed elements have equal ratings, generally speaking the local authorities prefer those that are prefabricated in the factory to those that are made on site because the timbers are more protected from damp. They contend that it is not possible to maintain factory conditions on site and the timbers are likely to pick up moisture and in time deteriorate, however careful the builder may be.

The normal atmospheric moisture content of timber is 17–22 per cent and a borough surveyor may well stipulate a 12 per cent moisture content in the timber used in a house. A builder who allows it to rise to as much as 30 per cent runs the risk of having his houses condemned by the local authority and he will be compelled to pull them down. This actually happened in a South London borough, where the builder had allowed the timber to remain exposed for too long. This is no problem for the experienced builder, who orders the timber to be delivered with the correct percentage moisture content in stages as work progresses instead of in one bulk delivery. But in general the phenomenal speed at which factory-produced houses are assembled on site reduces the traditional hazards from weather to a minimum. For this reason local authorities are increasingly turning to timber-frame houses to solve their housing problems, in which case they are responsible for site development.

Where a private builder is concerned, it is necessary to apply to the local planning authority for permission to build, at the same time submitting a detailed plan of the proposed development. The manufacturer, however, may be prepared to undertake these preliminary negotiations on behalf of his client.

Hazards Eliminated

Many of the traditional hazards of old-time timber building have been recognised and overcome at the design stage of a house. Building regulations have become increasingly stringent of late years and architects are compelled to incorporate safeguards against fire in their designs and builders must take certain precautions against rot and decay in timbers.

Most timber comes into the builders' hands already seasoned and needs no drying out, but to guard against decay the sill plate is automatically treated with preservative and tests are made to ensure that the moisture content of the timber is well below 20 per cent before it is sealed in. Because of the dry construction of the house no structural timbers need be treated as a general rule, but in certain areas where the house longhorn beetle lives, more particularly the Surrey–Hampshire borders, it is laid down that all roof timbers must be treated against pest. The advanced techniques of modern timber-framing allows for all these safeguards to be built in and so the local authorities are satisfied in every respect.

Fire Risks Overcome

The fear of fire has been one of the main objections to timber building, but it is better described as a misconception, for in the last analysis it is the *contents* of a house which constitute the risk and any house, whatever its method of construction, is liable to the same risk. Nevertheless, modern designers recognise the fact that timber is a combustible material and faithfully observe all local and national fire regulations to make their buildings fireproof. By the use of incombustible linings the timber structure is given a fire resistance which is more than adequate for safety.

Practical tests carried out at the Fire Research Station in collaboration with the Timber Research and Development Association have been very satisfactory and reassuring. Furnace tests determined the degree of fire resistance of various types of surface protection, but the Building Regulations and British Standard Fire Tests make a clear distinction between fire resistance, resistance to flamespread, and the idea of being non-combustible. The most important point here is resistance to flamespread and this is effectively achieved by a surface coating of salts or impregnation, and once this is done the other factors are of little account.

It is a fact that there is now more fire risk with some of the plastic materials and asbestos, which explode when they reach a certain degree of heat, than there is with timber.

It was not until 1966 that many local authorities and building societies withdrew their objections to timber-frame houses because of fire risks. Then new Building Regulations were introduced which allowed this kind of building to proceed without hindrance from authority. In London there were separate regulations and it was not until 1968 that the first large factory-made industrialised estate was built for a local authority in the London area, at Bedford Hill, Balham (Plate 38). Others have since followed and have proved their worth. For the local authorities it means shorter waiting-lists for houses and quicker slum clearance; for the private house builder it makes for speedier completion and earlier occupation. Insurance companies are prepared to offer comprehensive rates comparable with those for traditional houses and building societies rarely raise difficulties, usually regarding this method of construction as a sound mortgage risk. It is indeed the method of the future.

Into the Future
The very latest development in the field of industrialised timber-frame building is a three-dimensional system pioneered by Kingsberry Homes Ltd. The house, precision built, with all its wiring,

plumbing, central heating, kitchen, and bathroom installed in the factory, is delivered to the prepared site in two main box sections, ready to be lowered on to the foundations and linked together by infill panels. A builder locates the roof trusses, tiles the roof, and puts on the cladding, completing all site work in a few days. Even the wall coverings are on and the carpets ready to lay before this pre-packaged home leaves the factory, all but the essential on-site jobs having been transferred to the production line.

Though these houses are more standardised than the other types already described, the manufacturers offer such a wide choice of design that there can be few objections on that score. Initially applied to bungalows, the method was favourably received by the public at the 1970 Ideal Home Exhibition in London. It has the full approval of the leading building societies and insurance companies and can be erected by any builder approved by the National House Builders Registration Council. The price compares very favourably with other systems of timber-frame building, and all things considered this system may well complete the swing of public opinion back to timber-framing.

So timber has come into its own again. The process of evolution has taken us from a rough shelter of brushwood through many stages of leisurely hand-wrought craftsmanship in building to the present-day prefabricated and 'packaged' house erected at speed for people who are on the threshold of the space age. In each era, the buildings have expressed the mood of the age, the unfolding of the social history of a nation, and each has its rightful place in the story of the English timber-frame house.

Appendix

The professional bodies and trade organisations listed below will put enquirers in touch with local members for restoration work or new building. Full details of requirements should be given.

For Information on Timber
Timber Research and Development Association
Hughenden Valley, High Wycombe, Buckinghamshire

Timber Trade Federation of the United Kingdom
Clareville House, Whitcomb Street, London, WC2

The British Wood Preserving Association
6 Southampton Place, London, WC1

The British Woodwork Manufacturers' Association
Carrington House, 130 Regent Street, London, W1

Council of the Forest Industries of British Columbia
(Timber-Frame Housing Group)
Templar House, 81 High Holborn, London, WC1

Specialist Architects
Royal Institute of British Architects
66 Portland Place, London, W1N 4AD

Specialist Surveyors
Royal Institution of Chartered Surveyors
12 Great George Street, London, SW1

Builders
Federation of Master Builders
33 John Street, Holborn, London, WC1
National Federation of Building Trades Employers
82 New Cavendish Street, London, W1

Rural Craftsmen (wrought-iron smiths, thatchers, etc)
Council for Small Industries in Rural Areas
  (Advisory Services Division)
35 Camp Road, Wimbledon Common, London, SW19

Craftsmen in Building Trades
Incorporated British Institute of Certified Carpenters
37 Soho Square, London, W1
The Plasterers' Craft Guild
(Hon Secretary) 60 Chatto Road, London, SW11
Guild of Bricklayers
(Secretary) 37 Stockton Road, London, N18
Guild of Architectural Ironmongers
52–4 High Holborn, London, WC1
Associated Master Plumbers and Domestic Engineers
81 Gower Street, London, WC1
National Federation of Roofing Contractors
West Bar Chambers, 38 Boar Lane, Leeds, LS1 5DE, Yorkshire
National Master Tile Fixers Association
32 Queen Anne Street, London, W1
National Association of Roofing Tile Manufacturers
Grove House, Sutton New Road, Birmingham 23, Warwickshire

Interior Design
Incorporated Institute of British Decorators and Interior Designers
30 Baker Street, London, W1M 2DS

For Guidance on Legislation
The Society for the Protection of Ancient Buildings
55 Great Ormond Street, London, WC1

The Council for the Protection of Rural England
4 Hobart Place, London, SW1

The Ministry of Housing and Local Government
Whitehall, London, SW1

Permanent Exhibition of Building Materials and Information Centre
The Building Centre
26 Store Street, Tottenham Court Road, London, WC1

Principal County Archaeological Societies

Architectural and Archaeological Society of Durham and Northumberland
Prebends' Gate, Quarry Heads Lane, Durham
Bedfordshire Archaeological Council
Luton Museum, Wardown Park, Luton, Bedfordshire
Berkshire Archaeological Society
(Hon Secretary) 32 Eton Road, Datchet, Buckinghamshire
Buckinghamshire Architectural and Archaeological Society
c/o Museum, Church Street, Aylesbury, Buckinghamshire
Middle Thames Archaeological and Historical Society
(Hon Secretary) 38 Elmwood Road, Slough, Buckinghamshire
Chester Archaeological Society
c/o Public Library, St John Street, Chester
Cornwall Archaeological Society
(Hon Secretary) 'Bosgea', Steeple Lane, St Ives, Cornwall
Cumberland and Westmorland Antiquarian and Archaeological Society
Tullie House, Castle Street, Carlisle, Cumberland
Devon Archaeological Exploration Society
c/o Museum, Queen Street, Exeter, Devon
Dorset Natural History and Archaeological Society
Dorset County Museum, High Street West, Dorchester, Dorset
Essex Archaeological Society
(Hon Secretary) Cranford House, Elmstead, Colchester, Essex

Bristol and Gloucestershire Archaeological Society
Council House, Bristol 1, Gloucestershire

City of London Archaeological Society
(Hon Secretary) 131 Evering Road, London, N16

London and Middlesex Archaeological Society
Bishopsgate Institute, Bishopsgate, London, EC2

Hampshire Field Club and Archaeological Society
(Hon Secretary) Department of Archaeology, The University of
   Southampton, Hampshire

East Hertfordshire Archaeological Society
c/o Museum, Bull Plain, Hertford

Watford and South-West Hertfordshire Archaeological Society
Watford Central Library, Hampstead Road, Watford, Hertfordshire

Kent Archaeological Society
Museum, St Faith's Street, Maidstone, Kent

Record Society of Lancashire and Cheshire
(Hon Secretary) Lancashire Record Office, Sessions House, Lancaster
   Road, Preston, Lancashire

Leicestershire Archaeological and Historical Society
Guildhall, Guildhall Lane, Leicester

Lincolnshire Local History Society (including the Lincolnshire
   Architectural and Archaeological Society)
86 Newland, Lincoln

Norfolk and Norwich Archaeological Society
36 St Alban's Road, Norwich, Nor 26C, Norfolk

Oxfordshire Archaeological Society
c/o Ashmolean Museum, Oxford

Stamford and Rutland Archaeological and Local History Society
(Hon Secretary) 'Rowsley', Ryhall, Stamford, Lincolnshire

Shropshire Archaeological Society
c/o Borough Library, Shrewsbury, Shropshire

Somerset Archaeological and Natural History Society
Taunton Castle, Taunton, Somerset

Suffolk Institute of Archaeology
Record Office, 8 Angel Hill, Bury St Edmunds, Suffolk

Surrey Archaeological Society
Castle Arch, Guildford, Surrey

Sussex Archaeological Society
Barbican House, Lewes, Sussex

Coventry and District Archaeological Society
(Hon Secretary) 3 Shortley Road, Whitley, Coventry, Warwickshire

Wiltshire Archaeological and Natural History Society
Museum, 40–41 Long Street, Devizes, Wiltshire

Worcestershire Archaeological Society
The Greyfriars, Friar Street, Worcester

Yorkshire Archaeological Society
10 Park Place, Leeds 1, Yorkshire

Cardiff Archaeological Society
(Hon Secretary) c/o 62 Ryder Street, Cardiff, Glamorgan

The Radnorshire Society
(Hon Secretary) c/o County Hall, Llandrindod Wells, Radnorshire

In addition to the above, there are a great number of local archaeological and historical societies. They are always helpful and cooperative in other people's problems concerning old houses. Their addresses may be obtained from a local public library or the nearest county library.

Acknowledgements

We are grateful for leave to quote from: *Building in England Down to 1540* by L. F. Salzman, by permission of the publishers, The Clarendon Press, Oxford; *The English Farmhouse and Cottage* by M. W. Barley, by permission of Routledge & Kegan Paul Ltd; *Old English Houses* by Hugh Braun, by permission of Faber & Faber Ltd; 'The Houses of Radnorshire' by Henry Brooksby, from *The Transactions of The Radnorshire Society*; the records of the East Herts Archaeological Society; and to Mr David Kaye, directing research on behalf of the Gentlemen's Society of Spalding, for permission to publish his findings.

We also thank the many professional bodies, commercial organisations, and individuals who granted us facilities and assisted us in our research, particularly the following: the timber trades organisations (listed in the appendix), the Forests Products Research Laboratory, the Director of Avoncroft Museum, the Weald and Downland Open Air Museum, the Borough Architect and Planner of the London Borough of Southwark, the South Eastern Gas Board, the East Surrey Water Company, the Advisory Services Division of the Council for Small Industries in Rural Areas, William J. Bushby Ltd (Building Contractors), All Hallows Berkyngechirche by the Tower, Mr Gordon Moodey, Mr J. R. Armstrong, MA, Mr R. H. Wood, Mr John Smith, Mr J. Burchell, Mr J. Cunningham, Lt Col J. M. Langley, Mr J. King, Mr D. Searle, Mr and Mrs F. W. Rings, Dr and Mrs F. Harwood Stevenson, Mr and Mrs J. Brock, Mr and Mrs E. Maidment, Mr and Mrs A. Harrison, Mrs A. Davis, Mr and Mrs E. H. Doe, Mr A. McKechnie, Miss Cook, Mr and Mrs C. Mytton-Davies, Mr and Mrs A. Perkins, Mr and Mrs W. E. Townsley, and others who have assisted us by various means including permission to inspect and photograph their homes.

Index